D1035247

TRAVELLING BY SEA
IN THE NINETEENTH CENTURY

By the same authors

Westcountrymen in Prince Edward's Isle
(American Association for State and Local History Award of Merit, 1968)
The Merchant Sailing Ship: A photographic history
Women Under Sail

By Basil Greenhill

The Merchant Schooners (2 vols)
Sailing for a Living
Boats and Boatmen of Pakistan

By Rear Admiral P. W. Brock and Basil Greenhill

Steam and Sail

387.542
G-83

11.58

Travelling by Sea in the Nineteenth Century

INTERIOR DESIGN IN VICTORIAN PASSENGER SHIPS

Basil Greenhill,

Director of the National Maritime Museum

and Ann Giffard

HASTINGS HOUSE PUBLISHERS
NEW YORK, 10016

68181

First published in USA 1974 by
Hastings House, Publishers.
Originally published by
A. & C. Black Limited.

© 1972 Basil Greenhill and Ann Giffard

Dedicated to
B. J. GREENHILL
who inculcated
a love of social history

LIBRARY OF CONGRESS CATALOGING IN PUBLICATION DATA
Greenhill, Basil:
Travelling by sea in the nineteenth century.
1. Merchant ships—Passenger accommodation—
History. 2. Ocean travel—History. I. Giffard, Ann,
joint author. II. Title.
HE599.G73 1974   387.5'42'09034   74–19146
ISBN 0–8038–7151–1

All rights reserved. No part of this publication may
be reproduced, stored in a retrieval system or
transmitted, in any form or by any means,
electronic, mechanical, photocopying, recording or
otherwise, without the prior permission of
Hastings House, Publishers, Inc.

Printed photolitho in Great Britain by
J. W. Arrowsmith Ltd, Bristol.

Acknowledgement is made to the following publishers and authors for permission to quote from their books. David & Charles: *The Last Days of Mast and Sail* by Sir Alan Moore; *Mayflower Remembered* by Crispin Gill; *Women Under Sail* by Basil Greenhill and Ann Giffard. Hodder and Stoughton Ltd.: *Sons of Sinbad* by Alan Villiers. Hurst and Blackett Ltd.: *The Memoirs of William Hickey* edited by Alfred Spencer. Travel Book Club, and the original publisher whose name we have been unable to trace: *Through Mighty Seas* by Henry Hughes.

The following acknowledgements are made to the sources of the plates:

The Viking Ship Museum, Roskilde, Denmark, Plate 1

The National Maritime Museum, Stockholm, Plates 2, 31

Basil Greenhill, Plates 3, 9, 28

The Manx Museum, Isle of Man, Plate 4

The National Maritime Museum, Plates, 5, 6, 8, 14, 15, 16, 17, 18, 19, 20, 21, 29, 30, 32, 33, 34, 35, 40, 41, 42, 43, 44, 45, 46, 47, 48, 49, 50, 51, 52, 53, 54, 55, 56, 57, 58, 59, 60, 61, 62, 63, 64, 65, 66, 67, 68, 69, 70, 71, 72, 77, 78

The Peabody Museum of Salem, Mass., Plates 7, 26, 27

The Canterbury Museum, Christchurch, N.Z., Plates 10, 11, 12, 13

Mystic Seaport, Conn., Plates 22, 23, 24, 25

Robert Weinstein, San Francisco, Plate 36

The Trade and Shipping Museum, Elsinore, Denmark, Plate 37

The B.P. Bishop Museum, Honolulu, Plates 38, 39

The Maritime Museum at Fall River, Mass., Plates 73, 74

The Shelburne Museum, Vt., Plates 75, 76

CONTENTS

PART ONE
THE SAILING SHIP

CHAPTER ONE

Living at Sea Before the Nineteenth Century

The development of the boat to the point at which a complete permanent deck was fitted, turning the boat into a vessel and providing covered accommodation for some of the people who travelled on board, came at widely separated periods in time in different societies all over the world. For thousands of years men and women made long voyages in boats which were either open or at the best only partly or temporarily decked. Such were the vessels of Homeric Greece, so must have been the unknown boats in which Bronze Age travellers moved up the western coasts of Europe. The Polynesian Islands of the Pacific were populated by a series of open boat voyages, the majority probably accidental, spread over a long period of time, covering great distances and carrying in total many hundreds of men and women. Rugged as conditions must have been for these travellers, they were better off than their later contemporary open boat voyagers in the cold, wet, unpredictable climate of Northern Europe. These were the Vikings.

These great travellers, men, women, children and their livestock, moved between Scandinavia and the Eastern Mediterranean on the one hand and Greenland and Newfoundland on the other, in boats with no permanent protection against the weather. Natural selection both at sea and in the rigorous conditions of life ashore must have produced a race conditioned to survive, but the problem of how they did continue to live and retain the high level of physical energy necessary to row and sail big open boats in the face of continuous exposure to bad weather has not yet been adequately studied. Contemporary accounts by Muslim travellers of one Viking group, the Swedish Rus of the Volga, describe a people whose way of life was well adapted to the conditions of open boat voyaging – total lack of privacy, of sanitation and perpetual shortage of water. Ibn Fadlan wrote in a well-known tenth century account:

'They are the filthiest of God's creatures. They do not wash after discharging their natural functions, neither do they wash their hands after meals. They are as stray donkeys. They arrive from their distant lands and lay their ships alongside the banks of the Atul, which is a great river, and there they build big wooden houses on its shores. Ten or twenty of them may live together in one house, and each of them has a couch of his own where he sits and diverts himself with the pretty slave girls whom he has brought along to offer for sale. He will make love with one of them in the presence of his comrades, sometimes this develops into a communal orgy . . . Every morning a girl brings her master a large bowl of water in which he washes his face and hands and hair, combing it also over the bowl, then blows his nose and spits into the water . . . when he has finished the girl takes the same bowl to his neighbour who repeats the performance – until the bowl has gone round the entire household. All have blown their noses, spat and washed their faces and hair in the water.'

For centuries after the Viking era, open boats remained a normal method of travel. Passengers were carried in open boats across the Bristol Channel, the Irish Sea, the English Channel even at its widest, across the North Sea and to the outlying islands of Scotland. Country families established on the seaboard had their own boats, just as they had carts and carriages, and they used the boats in the same way as they used the land vehicles. For the Quayles of Castletown, Isle of Man, for example, in the 1790s the normal vehicle in which they travelled to the mainland – Liverpool, North Wales or the North Lancashire coast – was one of the small fleet of family boats, the largest of which was 26 feet long. In these boats were carried letters and, the surviving family records show, such items as a cask of tar and a tar mop, two large box smoothing irons, two dozen collars and a large door lock, as well as passengers. Almost miraculously one of these boats, the largest, named the *Peggy,* has survived and is now in the Nautical Museum at Castletown, Isle of Man, a part of the Manx Museum.

Even in the late nineteenth century prosperous seaboard families used their own boats to reach nearby centres, while for the ordinary man and woman the open boat was still the only means of travel between seaboard and island settlements. The Tyackes of Merthen Manor, near Constantine in Cornwall, would sometimes begin a journey to London by sailing in their small working ketch, the *Rob Roy,* to catch the train at Plymouth. The *Rob Roy,* built in 1882, was decked apart from a big hatchway. In the eighteenth century the same family would have travelled, like the Quayles, by open boat.

Open boat voyaging still persists in the modern world in the Indian Ocean and parts of the Western Pacific. These are voyages made in relatively favourable climatic conditions. I have myself seen open boats crowded with passengers in the Bay of Bengal bound along the coast of East Pakistan. Alan Villiers described the circumstances of an open boat passage in which he took part in 1939 in the Indian Ocean in his unique account of Arab sailing, *Sons of Sinbad.*

'The *Sheikh Mansur* was run very simply. Without any kind of windlass, and no anchor save a grapnel and a piece of stone in which a spike had been embedded; with no boat other than a small dugout canoe; with no instruments or aids to navigation beyond one decrepit, hopeless, and largely invisible boat compass dating back at least a century; without even a leadline to sound, she somehow wandered along cheerfully, and she had been sailing like that for at least thirty years . . . She had no shelter, no decks, no charts, no bell, no barometer, no clock. What need was there for shelter, when it it never rained? Why have decks, when no sea broke on board? Who needed charts, when Ahmed knew every reef and every headland, every strip of beach and every rock by eye, from long and close personal association? What need was there of bells and clocks, when time was not a passing torrent to be vainly measured?'

Alan Villiers, 'Sons of Sinbad', London, 1940

These are the conditions and attitudes of mind which have applied to most travellers by sea in the long history of man until the nineteenth century.

Sir Alan Moore charmingly described another comparatively modern open boat voyage made during World War I.

'In October 1918 we were lying at Stavros, and one day a boat came alongside manned by four monks in brimless tall hats. They had come from Mount Athos, and were taking corn and oil to some people farther up the coast who were starving, as many were at that time. The visit brought home strongly the physical and economical differences between that country and England. It was as though some monks of Quarr Abbey near Ryde had manned a little boat in Wooten Creek and had set out under oars and sails to carry food to people in distress at Broadstairs, calling on a man of war belonging to a distant power lying in Dungeness East Roads; and wearing tall hats all the time.'

Sir Alan Moore, 'The Last Days of Mast and Sail', Newton Abbot, 1970

In British seas open-boat sailing for a living is a very different matter. Yet it persisted in the fishing industry. It was only in the course of the nineteenth century that, with increasing population, better communications ashore and more demand for fish, the industry became prosperous enough to finance the use of relatively large, decked vessels for the longer range fisheries. The inshore business employed open sailing and rowing boats until well into this century. Stephen Reynolds, who lived and worked with South Devon fishermen only seventy years ago described their way of life as going to hell not for the experience but 'just barely to live'. Here is his account of part of a night's open boat work.

'The night wore on. We hauled in our nets, picked out a thousand or so of herrings, and shot again. We finished our food and our tea, squatted down and with coats over our heads we tried very hard to sleep. All our old clothes were damp; the bow-sheets, on which we lay, were soaking with water and fish slime, and underneath them some dirty bilge water, which we had had no time to clean out, stank like drains. I jammed myself under the cutty, in the warm; but oilskins over damp clothes, making one itch like forty thousand fleas, turned me out again into the cold.'

Stephen Reynolds, 'Seems So', London, 1908

Discomfort, squalor, and hardship in sea travel persisted long after decked vessels became normal for cargo and passenger carrying. The conditions were, of course, complementary to those in the country ashore. Most merchant ships were small until well into the eighteenth century. Passengers were carried in numbers which reflect standards of living quite remote from those of Western Europe and North America today. Like the third class carriages of an Indian train, the vessel often provided transport and nothing more. There was usually space for each passenger to lie down, but by no means necessarily all under cover. The ship provided water and a cooking fire for communal use, buckets for sanitation but often nothing else. To take the classic case of the *Mayflower's* voyage in 1620, there were 102 men, women and children packed into roughly 1,800 square feet. Since the space was by no means free of obstructions this means each had less than the area of a small sofa as their living space for a two-month's North Atlantic passage in a vessel which, like many wooden ships, leaked continuously through the decks. Crispin Gill sums up the conditions of sea travel for the passengers very well:

'Probably they slept, whole families together, in their own blankets and on their own straw mattresses, on the bare decks. They had victualled collectively, and what little cooking they could do was by families on the little brick oven in the fore-peak, or on charcoal stoves in the tiller flat. They were so crowded that some even slept in the shallop. The time from leaving Leyden to the final move ashore in New England must have seemed interminable . . . 244 days or 8 months.'

Crispin Gill, 'Mayflower Remembered', Newton Abbot, 1970

There was no question of cabin, saloon or even steerage in the nineteenth century sense, no furniture and no fittings, absolutely no interior decoration. Even the professional master and mate had little more than the hutch-like berths, built into the sides of the after cabin in which they slept, and room to stow sea chests and a table to eat off. The crew, like the passengers, berthed where they could on the decks and had no permanent place of their own. A complete and convincing picture of conditions of life at sea in a first class warship contemporary of the *Mayflower*, but very much larger, has been provided by the finds in the *Wasa*, built and lost in 1628 and raised a few years ago from the bottom of the sea for preservation in Stockholm. The officers had small cabins with simple bunks at one level or another in the five-storeyed square stern of the vessel. The petty officers had deck space of their own with only 5 feet of headroom. Here they slept and had their tiny piece of private living.

Seeing these little hutches one can understand the comment of Edward Barlow who first went to sea in a comparable British warship in 1659. Of his first night on board he wrote:

'And the night being come, my master and mistress and I went aboard; and that night I was put into a cabin to sleep, a thing much like some gentleman's dog kennel, for I was forced to crawl in upon all fours, and when I was in and set upon my breech I could not hold my head upright; but being very weary I slept indifferently well.'

Barlow's Journal, Original in the National Maritime Museum

The seamen and supernumeraries of the *Wasa*, about 400 of them, slept on the deck. The cooking place was an open brick hearth which could by no means always be used. A good deal of the personal equipment of the sailors has been found, sea chests with drinking kegs, wooden spoons, crude sandals, sewn cloth stockings. The limited resources on board are underlined by the equipment the men found it necessary to take with them, the shoe repairing gear, the simple pottery bowls, glazed on the inside only and held by looped handles which, together with the wooden spoons and round wooden platters, were all the eating equipment a seaman ever handled. The officers ate off their personal pewter. The captain's table, one of the few pieces of furniture found on board, has been reconstructed. It is a rough three-planked table and on it have been assembled earthenware and pewter plates, a two-pronged iron fork, a pewter tankard, a bronze brazier used to keep a bowl of soup warm and bronze candlesticks, all discovered in the vessel and probably comprising much of the table's original equipment. A silver spoon provides almost the only touch of luxury.

Of course, the *Wasa* was lost at the beginning of her maiden voyage before she had been properly fitted out or fully manned, but the finds in her underline the simplicity of life at sea in the early 1600s. A fully-commissioned warship or a large merchant ship would have had a great deal more on board her, but it would have been largely the personal property of her officers and would have represented their taste and wealth on land. The furniture the rich took with them to sea was part of their land furniture. The ordinary man and woman had little but a space to lie down.

This situation was to continue for upwards of two centuries. This was, of course, still an era when ordinary people travelled very little. There was certainly no extensive movement of passengers on long sea voyages. Passengers crossed to the Continent in fair numbers, but these were brief passages in vessels quite often chartered from ordinary trading or fishing for the purpose. A relatively large number of people crossed the Atlantic to settle in North America, but though the ships became some-what larger and more efficient, the bulk of the migrants travelled under conditions not very different from the passengers in the *Mayflower*. The rich took their comforts with them.

This tradition, that the ship provided the space and the minimum of essentials and the passenger brought, or did not bring, the rest of his comforts from the shore, died very hard and we shall see that in fact vestiges of it persisted until well into the nine-teenth century. In the late 1700s, conditions on board a big East Indiaman bound for Bombay or Calcutta were such that the prosperous and well-equipped passenger could have quite a pleasant time by the standards of his day, though even by these standards the voyage must have been a tedious affair. The expansion of British influence and administration in India in the eighteenth century meant that this was a part of the world to which people travelled in fair numbers. Army officers, merchants, civil administrators, the employees of the merchants, adventurers and their women, and other women who sought husbands from among the bachelor community, made the passage to India. Far fewer came back.

The captain of an Indiaman had a number of privileges by the judicious use of which he could build up a fortune large enough to enable him to set himself up in a gentle-man's style ashore at a relatively early age. One of these perquisites was the fares of the passengers to whom he hired out the space in the ship's after accommodation. In return for considerable sums the passengers received little more than private deck space, a roof over their heads, a seat at the table and the food and drink they consumed there. In 1764 Colonel Champion was willing to pay 2,000 rupees in return for which he was provided with a compartment wide enough to embrace two of the windows built into the broad stern of the ship. Everthing in the way of equipment he had to provide for himself. When William Hickey sailed for India in 1777 he had to share his expensive cabin with three other men and to pay the captain 100 guineas for the privilege of eating at his table. The really rich would hire the complete after cabin and partly furnish it or take half of it and the deckhouse as well. Captain Eastwick, writing of a discussion he had had in 1791 with the owner of an Indiaman, when he himself was contemplating joining the India trade, described the system by which the Captain benefited from passage money:

'In addition to the free tonnage, he further enjoyed certain advantages in the carrying of passengers, for although the allowance of passage money outward and homeward was arbitrarily fixed by the company, there being a certain number of passengers assigned to each vessel, and their fares duly determined, ranging from £95 for a subaltern and assistant surgeon to £235 for a general officer, with from one and a half to three and a half tons of free baggage, exclusive of bedding and furniture for their cabins, yet it was possible for captains by giving up their own apartments and accommodation to make very considerable sums for themselves. In short the gains to a prudent commander averaged from £4,000 to £5,000 a voyage, sometimes perhaps falling as low as £2,000, but at others rising to £10,000 and £12,000. The time occupied from the period of the ship commencing receipt of her outward cargo to her being finally cleared of her homeward one was generally from fourteen to eighteen months, and three or four voyages assured any man a very handsome fortune.'

R. W. Eastwick, A Master Mariner, London, not dated

The stern cabin of the late eighteenth century merchant vessel was the site of the most costly and the most commodious accommodation. If the vessel was very large there were several such cabins at different levels. Some impression of what this accommodation must have been like in the largest merchant vessels can be gained on board H.M.S. *Victory* in Portsmouth Dockyard, or in the *Constitution* at Boston Navy Yard. But, of course, only the greatest of Indiamen had accommodation remotely to compare with these grandeurs. The average merchant ship at the beginning of the nineteenth century was a vessel of a couple of hundred tons, but in these vessels also the stern cabin could be made very comfortable. Nearly all stern cabins had a common characteristic, the stern windows, two, four, six or eight of them, which provided light and ventilation to a degree and with a convenience not obtainable elsewhere in the ship. Below them was a deep sill made by the curving in of the counter of the vessel underneath. Between them in the centre was the box-like structure of the rudder trunk, above them the beams curved to the camber of the poop deck, the underside of which formed the ceiling of the cabin in a small vessel. Underfoot the deck was cambered also.

We have described this stern cabin at some length because the pattern described above was to be the dominant feature of a cabin passenger's sea life until the middle of the nineteenth century, and the chief feature of the accommodation of merchant ships throughout the period. Sometimes this accommodation was left as an open space. In passenger ships it was more frequently divided, as in the vessel in which Colonel Champion bought his passage. Sometimes the divisions were entirely temporary, even made of canvas. Sometimes they were semi-permanent. When in 1796 Dr Pinckard sailed to Barbados he found that his ship, the *Lord Sheffield,* had permanent apartments and sleeping berths, a large cabin fitted with a mahogany wainscot and a sofa and reasonable ventilation. For male passengers there were bathing tubs on deck. Females were not able to bath during the whole passage. All these unusual features were matters of note to the seasoned sea traveller. But a West Indiaman carried less than a dozen passengers, an East Indiaman might carry four times as many.

The rest of the accommodation, if any, of a merchant ship in the late eighteenth century was provided in one of the deck houses on the poop, in cabins in the forward part of the poop so small that one 6 feet by 7 was considered good accommodation, and in cabins below the main stern cabin in a big vessel. The rest was the 'steerage', by which was usually meant empty cargo space offering quarters little different from those in which the Pilgrim Fathers had travelled. It was in such accommodation that the bulk of the travellers who emigrated to North America in the seventeenth and eighteenth centuries were carried.

Later, partly at least because in this way many more people could be packed into a vessel, two- or three-tiered bunks were built on the intermediate cargo decks (usually only one) of lightly laden westbound vessels. It was in these conditions that many of the Highlanders travelled who, as sheep farming moved slowly northwards, left Scotland for the New World in the later part of the eighteenth century. That these travellers had nothing but a space to lie down in is vividly demonstrated by the fact that in 1773 a vessel of 100 tons carried 450 passengers, of whom 25 were without even sleeping space until deaths created 23 vacancies. The rest had 2 square feet of deck space each for the voyage. Eighteen years later a 270-ton ship is reported to have taken on board no less than 400 passengers. The three-tier berths were $1\frac{1}{2}$ feet wide and had 2 feet of headroom. Of course, as in the emigrant ships of the middle nineteenth century, men and women lived together in these conditions.

A great many Irish emigrants were carried to North America in similar conditions in the late eighteenth century. Just as in the Great Migration which followed after 1830, the empty timber ships returning to load more cargoes in North America provided cheap passages for would-be settlers by the thousand, so in the eighteenth century the vessels which carried flax seeds to Ireland from New York City were ready to offer passenger transport at low rates on the westward passage, for Ireland offered few goods other than men and women for the American market. Compared with later years the numbers involved were of course small. One authority has stated that they probably did not exceed 5,000 in any single season in the eighteenth century. But in relation to the total number of people travelling overseas at the time, these and the Scots migrants of the same period represent very large numbers, perhaps the earliest example of the bulk movement of passengers across an ocean.

At the end of the eighteenth century, therefore, there were two trans-Ocean routes on which relatively large numbers of people were carried, across the North Atlantic in a westerly direction, and to India. Of those who crossed the seas the great majority travelled to North America in conditions of squalor, given no more than a place to lie down, a share in a bucket to relieve themselves in, some food or perhaps just somewhere to cook. A relatively few of the richer sort bound for North America had private space in the great cabin or in deck houses, and the majority of the much smaller numbers who travelled to India enjoyed these relatively luxurious conditions. For them the ship provided a private space with rudimentary fixtures, a place at a table and food. They had to bring their own cabin furniture with them. On short

9

passages, to the Continent or Ireland, there were regular packets which provided berths for the more prosperous. The rest travelled on deck, and probably the majority of travellers hired small cargo vessels, fishing vessels or open boats. All, on voyages long or short, shared a common circumstance: no laws, no Passenger Acts, governed the terms of their contracts and the conditions under which they were carried. Not until 1803 was the first of these Acts to result from the horrors of the Scottish emigrant trade to North America.

In the following hundred years a revolution in travel overseas was to take place at least as great as that which has occurred in our own time.

CHAPTER TWO

The Accommodation in Wooden Sailing Ships

The revolution in passenger transport at sea which took place in the nineteenth century left one class of vessel almost unaffected. The wooden sailing ship continued in use as a regular passenger carrier until the 1860s and, except for the Atlantic passage, the nature and standard of the service the majority of these vessels offered at the end of this period was much the same as at its beginning.

The ordinary medium-sized wooden vessel changed very little during these sixty and more years. At the end of them she remained pretty well what she had been. She had a massively built hull, flat underneath so that when she sat on the mud of a harbour at low tide (and many British ports of the period still had no floating dock facilities) she was able to remain upright. Her bows were full and round, she sailed slowly, pushing a great bow wave in front of her and she was very bad at sailing close to the wind. Her stern was square, the transom broken by stern windows to light the great cabin. Her masts were built up from massive wooden poles, each mast comprising three parts, joined with long overlaps. These masts were supported by a complex of rope, some of it latterly made of iron wire, called the standing rigging. This rigging required constant highly skilled attention to keep it in order. In bad weather the crew sent the upper sections of the masts – each section called a 'mast' in its own right, lower mast, topmast and topgallant mast – down to the deck, thereby reducing the wind resistance of the rigging and the turning moments of the great weights aloft.

With a skilled professional crew these vessels were safe, providing they did not meet extreme weather conditions and that they were kept in good condition and well-maintained. The largest of them, the biggest East-Indiamen, were of less than 2,000 tons. The ordinary merchant ship in general trade, which included the North Atlantic trade, was of 200 or 300 tons in the first quarter of the nineteenth century, increasing slowly to 500 or 600 in the 50s and 60s, although many smaller vessels were still built and many remained in service from the early years of the century. Such ships tended to ride like a cork on the great rollers of the Southern Ocean on their way from Cape Town to Australia and New Zealand. They shipped little water and in very bad weather they could drift more or less bows on to the wind for days on end in relative safety. They required constant pumping and they were prone to disaster from fire, from wreck following errors of navigation by masters and mates, and from the loss of masts and rigging as a result of neglect or bad judgment.

In these vessels two general classes of people travelled, the cabin passengers and the 'steerage'. The former occupied space in the stern cabin or sometimes, in larger vessels, immediately forward of it or in a deck house on the after deck. The latter had sleeping berths in the long 'tween decks, the space between the ordinary deck open to the weather and the next deck immediately below it – usually in small vessels there was only one covered deck. Cabin passengers brought their own furniture, steerage passengers rarely had any possessions beyond cooking and eating implements and anything that could be packed into a single chest. Indiamen did not take steerage passengers in the 'tween decks sense of the term and conditions in them were for most of the passengers as good as could be found at sea. In an Order of 1799, the Court of Directors of the East India Company urged their captains to pay proper attention to the treatment of passengers. 'The Diversity of Characters and Dispositions which must meet on shipboard makes some Restraint upon all necessary' . . . 'Anyone offending against good Manners or known Usages and Customs will, on Representation to the Court *(of the East India Company)* be severely noticed.' The use of fires in cabins was prohibited after 8 o'clock at night. Candles were to be extinguished by 9 o'clock except in the cabins where they could be kept alight until 10.

In 1808 William Hickey spent almost 30,000 rupees on his passage money and outfit for his voyage home to England from Calcutta in the *Castle Eden*. A good deal of this money went on the furniture of his cabin. This included the bed he slept in, a desk, a table and two large teakwood chests. His expensive cabin was, he found, tiny and low. He would have been lucky if it had been 12 feet square and if so it would have been one of the best cabins in the ship. The passengers who had occupied it during the *Castle Eden's* outward passage had removed all the furniture, which was their own property. Indeed, it was the custom on this particular journey, since it was almost always made in anticipation of a long stay in India, to equip the cabin with pieces which had been chosen for use in the home in Calcutta, Madras or Bombay. One woman writer advised that little more should be needed in the way of furniture in India over and above what was used to furnish the cabin on the outward passage – which implies the use of a certain amount of Indian-made furniture later on.

Half the 'round house', that is the deck house on the poop of an Indiaman of the 1820s, according to one contemporary correspondent advising future travellers, would be properly equipped if it contained a piano or harp, two or three small bureau with bookshelves on them, a 'wash-hand stand with two pewter juglets and two pewter basins', three chairs, a footbath and 'two or three sea couches with drawers to convert into sofas in the day time'. This particular writer, whose correspondents were young women, went on to say, 'nothing is so indelicate, indeed so indecent, as from the windows of the ladies' cabins to see anything towing overboard or being hung out to dry'.

In large vessels the relative merits of the great cabin in the stern, cabins forward of it under the poop and deck houses on the poop were a matter of dispute. The disadvantage of the great cabin was in bad weather. Airiness and comfort in the tropics was more than paid for by the violence of the motion at this extreme end of the vessel and the dangers of water coming through the plugged and barricaded windows in bad weather. When William and Matilda Johnstone sailed to Tasmania in 1841 they experienced bad weather for a whole month after setting out from London. What this meant can best be summed up in a single extract from William's journal of the voyage:

12

'On 18th, being in want of a candle, I cautiously opened the doors of the bookcase in which they were stowed away, when in an instant the whole contents, books, parcels, candles, etc, were saluting my head in a most unpleasant manner. Everything was turned out – all the exertions of myself and steward being insufficient to replace them, so much were we lying over – and we were compelled to leave them lying about on the floor. The only light in our cabin was admitted through a small bullseye in the deck, both our stern windows having deadlights up. Sleep at night was out of the question. The awful creaking of every part of the vessel, hollering of the sailors and roaring of the sea, with noises of every description, completely preventing it.'

Quoted in Basil Greenhill and Ann Giffard, 'Women Under Sail,' Newton Abbot, 1970

This question of noise was one of the factors in the relative merits of different kinds of accommodation. William Hickey did not like the stern cabin. He wrote:

'I have tried both (roundhouse and great cabin) and from that experience never would recommend any person to put himself between decks if accommodation can be had above. The objections to the roundhouse are the frequent noises that must occur upon the poop from the seamen performing the necessary manoeuvres with the sails attached to the mizen-mast . . . and the feeding of the poultry kept in coops there with the consequent pecking twice a day . . .

'But on the gun deck, if you avoid the noises above specified, they are more than counterbalanced by a variety of inconveniences, the great one that of being completely debarred of all daylight in tempestuous weather by what is ever expressively termed ''the deadlights'' being then fixed into all the windows, in order to prevent the sea breaking in; which nevertheless it does not effectually do, for I was often set afloat in my cabin by heavy seas breaking against those deadlights and entering at the seams, especially so at the quarter gallery door and windows, where it poured in in torrents beating even over my bed.'

William Hickey, 'Memoirs', London, 1949

Another passenger in a wooden sailing ship, a schooner of perhaps 150 tons, bound for St Michaels in the Azores from the west of England in the late 1830s wrote:

'Imagine a huge wicker basket of the driest materials, filled with heavy weights, suspended by each end, and put into rapid motion by being violently jerked backwards, forwards, and sidewards; and its creaking and screaming will very nearly resemble the grating of the new mahogany panelling in the cabin, which screeches so loudly and so incessantly as to drown all conversation. But this one unvarying noise is accompanied at regular intervals by the constant dull bumps of the heavy seas which continually strike the vessel in all parts. Now a stunning blow hits her on the bow, and a shower of spray sharply rattles against the cabin windows and drenches the decks; again and again the same dead blow, as from a stupendous wooden mallet, falling heavily on her, followed by the same drenching shower, seems to stun her and make her motionless in the water. For a moment hardly a sound is heard and she seems to have given up the contest in despair. Then the rolling and the pitching, the tossing and the creaking begin again, with the same vexatious violence. This ceaseless struggle between the vessel and the waves, with the shrill whistle of the gale through the strained rigging, a wild melancholy sound, as of a strange AEolian harp played by the tempest; the heavy fall of breaking waves and showers of spray; the splashing of the seas as they wash backwards and forwards on the deck; the muffled cry of the sailors in the storm; the sharp rap of blocks, and the incessant creaking of the new woodwork, make the weathering of gales of wind in a small schooner a rough piece of experience.'

Dr Butler, 'A Winter in the Azores', London 1841

Even in harbour the vessel was not free from the noises inevitably associated with a large wooden structure continuously subjected to varying stresses. When the vessels took the ground in the conditions illustrated in Plate 8 they creaked and groaned and every so often some timber would settle into place with a noise like a pistol shot. The same process happened all over again every time she floated off.

The passage from Hickey quoted above mentioned the poultry on the poop. Every sailing vessel, whether faced with a passage of from six weeks across the North Atlantic in a westerly direction or of three, four or five months bound towards India or Australia, was compelled to carry livestock. Cows and calves, sheep, goats, pigs and hens were carried in the larger vessels and the noises they made and the smells from their quarters did nothing to improve conditions. The hens were usually carried on the poop in order to protect them from the naturally thieving propensities of the crew, who would have left the passengers with few eggs if the hen coops had been readily accessible to them. Even the smallest vessel carried a few animals on voyages likely to be of any duration.

The smells were, of course, among the most notable features of life on board. The combination of animal and human excrement, foul water from the bottom of the ship below the pump wells which never came out, the remains of old cargoes and the perpetually rotting wooden structure of the vessel herself must between them have produced a dreadful stench, unrelieved by any kind of ventilation system in the ship. People were accustomed to this ashore in towns and villages which stank like an Oriental slum today, but occasionally the smells on shipboard became a matter of comment. One passenger in an East Indiaman, Robert Ramsay, notes in 1826, in the tropics: 'this heat, added to the closeness, made our cabins very oppresive; the foul air came up the hatchway in the form of smoke, and the captain even sent some one down to see whether the ship was not on fire'.

For the cabin passenger the food and eating conditions were often good by the standards of the times. In an East Indiaman everything was done with proper formality. At the beginning of the voyage passengers occupied the seats at table they had paid for, the two most senior ladies on each side of the captain. Humbler passengers ate in one of the spaces on the lower decks below the great cabin. The food served was as good as it could be bearing in mind the serving facilities available and the small farmyard the vessels carried. She probably carried a small market garden as well.

14

R. C. Leslie, recollecting his own passages in vessels in the North Atlantic trade in the 1840s, wrote:

> 'It was not unusual for the captain to do a little practical farming in the hold of his ship by planting out upon the freshly trimmed ballast cabbage, lettuce, spring onions, or any edible root that was likely to thrive in the soil he chanced to carry across the Atlantic with him. Most ships, some years back, had a small kitchen garden planted in boxes of earth in the jolly boat, which boat was further crammed to her gunwhales with green groceries of every sort; and, weather permitting this little garden was a source of great pleasure to a solitary skipper on a long voyage.'

R. C. Leslie, 'Old Sea Wings, Ways, and Words, in the Days of Oak and Hemp', London
1890

But it was not only in East Indiamen that food could be very satisfactory. On a passage to New Zealand in the bark *Blenheim* in 1840, Mrs Jessie Campbell reported:

> 'Forgot to mention the first pig was killed Saturday last, children had a roast of it on Sunday with which they were delighted . . . it was as delicate as lamb, so different from the pork on shore. . . . We are to have a sheep and pig killed every week, the pigs are very small; we have good soup every day and the children the same and fresh meat every day.'

Quoted in Basil Greenhill and Ann Giffard, 'Women Under Sail', Newton Abbot, 1970

A year later on their passage to Tasmania, Mr and Mrs William Johnstone shared the table in the great cabin with Captain Westmorland and five other persons, the chief officer, the doctor and three young male passengers. William Johnstone wrote: 'Our table was excellent, indeed our only want on board was milk – having no cow on board, and the goat perishing in the severe weather'. The *Arab*, the Johnstone's vessel, carried thirteen sheep, thirteen pigs, ten dozen fowls, a dozen geese and a dozen turkeys, two dozen ducks and the lamented goat, which meant that the eight people for whom these were provided dined well.

Passengers like the Campbells and the Johnstones enjoyed privacy – Johnstone wrote: 'we thoroughly enjoyed our little cabin, often spending eighteen hours out of the twenty-four therein', but nevertheless their accommodation was appallingly cramped by the standards of the late twentieth century. James and Fanny Fitzgerald travelled to New Zealand in 1850 on board the *Charlotte Jane*. Their half of the stern cabin, in the best position in the ship, cost them £42 each – perhaps the equivalent of £420 today. The cabin, which was on the starboard quarter and occupied half the width of the ship, was 11 feet wide and 9 feet long. Only one other cabin on board was as large. The Fitzgeralds, of course, had to supply their own furniture, bedding and all the other items needed to make daily life tolerable for a four month voyage. This furniture they had made for them, especially designed for the cabin and later to be used in their new home in New Zealand. They took with them a big double bed, a desk with turned wooden legs, candle lamps and a long, carved wooden easy chair with a cane back. There are in the Canterbury Museum, Christchurch, New Zealand, items brought by other passengers in the same and similar vessels: a single extension couch with cane back and end, a double extension couch with cane sides and back, a brass-bound cedar sea chest about 3 feet high with four drawers, a small cane-backed deck chair, a bedroom basin of glazed earthenware with underglazed blue transfer, a walnut work box and the stiffened cane and metal shapes on which women's dresses were made up.

The Fitzgeralds lived immediately under the poop deck and their cabin had three stern windows which when they were not barricaded against bad weather must have admitted a great deal of light and air. They also had the great privilege of the use of their own private lavatory, built into the starboard quarter gallery and accessible only from their cabin. Immediately forward of them were two staterooms, each measuring 8 feet by 6 and having space taken out of each of them for a small water closet which had to be shared. Not all the passengers liked this sharing, with results involving the use of chamber pots which could sometimes be unpleasant. Thus, Mrs Jessie Campbell wrote, 'Just as we were sitting to dinner felt a bad smell from J.B.S.'s cabin, strange they will not use our convenient closet.'

In the *Charlotte Jane* forward of the passenger's cabins, which were duplicated on the port side, was the main cabin with the thick shape of the mizzen mast coming down through it and a table athwartships where the cabin passengers ate with the master. They were served from a pantry and sideboard. Below was a lower deck with two stern cabins, each with only one window, and with four temporary partitioned cabins on each side of a central space where the passengers who lived on this deck (and who paid less passage money than the Fitzgeralds) ate with the mates of the vessel.

All the vessels to which we have been referring carried 'tween decks passengers, emigrants. Perhaps one of the most vivid references to this class of passenger was made by Mrs Jessie Campbell. Speaking of the master of the *Blenheim,* she recorded that he 'complains of the indolence and filthy habits of the Highlanders, the few Paisley emigrants keep themselves cleaner and are more easily managed'. William Johnstone found the emigrants in the *Arab* 'our greatest annoyance . . . a most awful set, about twenty respectable out of the whole number. Scenes are daily occuring, which though unnecessary to describe, are yet most revolting – and can scarcely be prevented. Fighting and swearing from morning till night . . . They were chiefly agricultural labourers from Somersetshire, who had been earning upon average 7s 6d a week, on which they supported their wives and families.'

It was, of course, this simplicity, this conditioning to a life without even the most rudimentary comforts, and the attendant freedom from complex anxieties which made possible the survival of the great majority of 'tween decks emigrants on the awful east-west passage across the North Atlantic and the long haul to Australia and New Zealand in small wooden sailing ships. For the conditions in which they travelled – seven and a half million across the North Atlantic alone between 1800 and 1875 – seem to late twentieth century eyes unimaginably dreadful.

For them there was no question of furniture. Emigrants lived in temporary communal dormitories built into the space between the main deck and a deck 5 or 6 feet below it. In the first half of the nineteenth century the 'tween decks were neither lit nor ventilated. Into this space were built rows of bunks, sometimes in three tiers and then, as the successive Passenger Acts demanded some improvement in conditions, in two tiers. These bunks were allocated each to a family, though a large family might get two. There was very little space between the tiers of bunks. Sanitation comprised buckets screened around and sometimes fitted with seats. There were no special washing places and water was rationed. This was a great hardship to any with fastidious tastes. Often the water was taken on board from the river in which the vessel lay before the beginning of the voyage and before long smelt foul and tasted worse. On board the barque *Civility*, of Bideford, Devon, bound for Canada in 1848, William Fulford, a 'tween decks passenger, wrote:

> '. . . our provisions are delivered to us from the store rooms on Mondays and Thursdays and our water every morning. This morning it was taken from a fresh cask, and it stank so that we could not drink it, so were obliged to boil it and put peppermint with it.'

In the early years of the century the food supply to emigrants was minimal and in some vessels had to be brought almost entirely by the passengers themselves. Even after the improvement of conditions, following upon legislation to protect passengers and the laying down of minimum supplies to be given to each passenger each week, there was scarcely any protein in the specified diet and it had to be supplemented by salt meat and fish brought by the passengers. In the *Civility*, William Fulford wrote on 10th April, 1848:

> 'The provisions we took with us we have found most useful, such as flour, as we can bake household bread every three days if we like for 1d a loaf; also a pie or pudding at $\frac{1}{2}$d each. There is an excellent cast iron oven and Boiler in the Galley and it belongs solely to the Cook (Ed Bale) who is an excellent Cook.
>
> 'Bat and Wm Shute might have sold their cider at a high price, $2\frac{1}{2}$ per pint if they would have disposed of it. We found everything we took most useful . . .
>
> 'I find my appetite rather delicate, which is unusual for me, but I am not surprised, as our sea biscuits contain so much horse bean flour, and our water is so impure that it produces indigestion. Never since I was born have I proved the value of good bread and the Western Well water at Buckland Brewer, its excellency and value, until deprived by the sea voyage.'

From a transcript in the possession of the authors

If you lived on 7s 6d a week in a cottage built of mud and straw with an earth floor and a thatched roof, relieving yourself at the bottom of the garden into a pit with a rough seat bench built over it, drawing your water from a well which might be several hundred yards away, and cooking your food on an open fire, the conditions described above were clearly not intolerable. And you could travel across the Atlantic for as little as £3 or at times, where there was a great number of vessels competing for passengers, for as little as 50p and buy your own food.

Most emigrants were people of no education introduced into an alien environment. They were superstitious and ignorant and they were hazarding themselves in a totally new way of life in a country of which they often had only the sketchiest knowledge.

17

The majority of them were agricultural workers and country craftsmen and before they gained the freedom and independence they sought they often had to undergo great hardships in a new and exceedingly hostile world. And there was no going back. As we have said elsewhere, the passage was a traumatic experience, less perhaps for its hardships than its strangeness and the finality of the step its taking represented.

There is no better description of an emigrant deck than one written on the arrival of the wooden bark *Airthy Castle* at Quebec in 1831. The *Airthy Castle* was about 100 feet long, considerably smaller than the sailing ship *Cutty Sark* now preserved near the National Maritime Museum at Greenwich.

'One forenoon I went on board the ship *Airthy Castle*, from Bristol, immediately after her arrival. The passengers were in number 254, all in the hold or steerage, all English, from about Bristol, Bath, Frome, Warminster, Maiden Bradley, etc. I went below, and truly it was a curious sight. About 200 human beings, male and female; young, old and middle-aged; talking, singing, laughing, crying, eating, drinking, shaving, washing, some naked in bed, and others dressing to go on shore; handsome young women (perhaps some), and ugly old men, married and single; religious and irreligious. Here a grave matron chanting selections from the last edition of the last new hymn book; there a brawny ploughboy "pouring forth the sweet melody of Robin Adair." These settlers were poor, but in general they were fine-looking people, and such as I was glad to see come to America. . . . It is my opinion that few among them will forget being cooped up below deck for four weeks in a moveable bedroom, with 250 fellow-lodgers as I have endeavoured to describe.'

Quoted in 'The Great Migration', 1968, National Maritime Museum

Some vessels remained in the emigrant trade across the North Atlantic for years and built up for themselves reputations as carriers providing the best conditions of travel possible in the circumstances. One such was the brig *Lord Ramsey*, built in Quebec in 1832 and owned by Thomas B. Chanter and other merchants in Bideford, North Devon. A contemporary note in the local newspaper gives an account of her which presents the emigrant ship's 'tween decks in the best possible light.

'Among the many vessels which have been prepared for the reception of emigrants there have been none fitted in such superior style and in so comfortable a manner as the fine brig *Lord Ramsey*, R. England, Master, now lying at Appledore bound to New York. The stanchions dividing the separate berths are elegantly turned and coloured and the whole has more the appearance of a comfortable hotel than a passenger ship. On deck there is a spacious cookhouse entirely for the use of passengers, and from the well known abilities and kind disposition of the Commander she will doubtless become a favourite vessel. We hear almost all the places in her are engaged.'

North Devon Journal, 1836

An account of a westerly crossing of the North Atlantic in the 'tween decks of a wooden sailing ship, the *Ocean Queen*, gives a graphic picture of the conditions under which emigrants had to exist in bad weather:

'Thursday, 12th. Weather dirty – about 4 p.m. orders were given to close-reef all sails as a storm was expected in half an hour every sail was furled and the ship pumped out, ready for the worst. By this time the rain had begun to fall and the wind to rattle through the ropes like thunder. This lasted but a few minutes, and we were all in hopes it was past over easily, but as it got dark the rain again began to fall, the wind to whistle and the sea to rise. By ten o'clock the storm was getting hot. Thunder is no more than a dog's bark compared with the tremendous roar of the wind and sea. Ten o'clock all but three passengers went below, to turn in and try to sleep, and I being the hindmost left the scuttle open, thinking the other three would follow. We had scarcely turned in when a sea struck her, making her reel most awfully. It came down the scuttle like a mill-stream, washing some of us nearly out of our beds. Two of our boxes broke from their lashings and rolled about from side to side, strewing their contents as they went.

'It was an anxious time; females shrieking, the water almost floating our things and the pails, can, etc, knocking about. It is impossible to convey an idea of such an awful sight. We had very little sleep this night.

'About 4 o'clock a.m. Friday there was a dead calm which lasted until about 7 a.m., when the storm recommenced with all its fury. The sailors on deck were obliged to be lashed as they could not stand. We could cook nothing today, but the steward brought us some coffee, etc, and the Capt comes down now and then to see us.

'I went to the top of the steps this morning, just to see the sea. I never witnessed such a sight before; it was one mass of foam, and rolling as high as our topmast, threatening every moment to swallow us up. About 2 p.m. another sea struck the ship, smashing in the cabin skylight and some of the bulwarks. This completed the disaster of last night. We were now fairly washed clean out. This appeared to be the height of the storm, for it began to abate, and, thank God, by his aid we were carried safely through it.'

> *Diary of W. Gliddon of Barnstaple, published as a broadsheet of the 'Western Standard', 1855. The 'Ocean Queen' was built at New Bideford, Prince Edward Island, Canada, for James Yeo in 1845, the master at the time of the passage described was Richard Dart.*

On these long voyages, six weeks from east to west across the North Atlantic, three or four months to Australasia, the modern passenger would be faced with interminable tedium. But in a world which moved as slowly as that of the first half of the nineteenth century conceptions of time were very different. The pace of life was set by the horse, the rowing boat, manual labour without machinery and in the home the slow processes of cooking on an open fire, sewing without a sewing machine, cleaning without detergents or ready hot water. In such a world time was of relatively little account. In the early part of the century a vessel bound for India might dawdle on her way with stops for weeks at Madeira and Cape Town. Later it sometimes took weeks to get through the tropics to the South Atlantic and a sailing vessel, especially a square-rigged sailing vessel, of course took the routes where the winds were most favourable because to do so was to save time and trouble in the end, even if it meant going thousands of miles out of the way.

During these voyages the cabin passengers entertained themselves with reading, playing cards and with the long drawn out afternoon dinner. The women sewed and looked after their children and both men and women wrote the dairies and journals and long letters, the chance survival of a few of which enables us to build up the picture of life here presented. The customs of the time and the probably unpleasant consequences of too easy contact with people who were intimate neighbours for weeks on end, led many passengers to adopt an attitude of considerable reserve towards their fellow travellers; families travelling together seem to have tended to keep their social lives to themselves except at table. The illiterate 'tween decks passengers kept to their bunks or simply talked interminably after the manner of such social groups anywhere in history. In a well-run vessel with a good master and crew, male 'tween decks passengers and even young men from the cabins could and did join readily in the working of the vessel to their own and everyone else's advantage. Craftsmen in the 'tween decks sometimes had the opportunity of exercising their skills after the vessel had been damaged in bad weather. On board the *Civility* William Fulford wrote on Monday, 17th April, 1848:

'I have not slept much tonight in consequence of the stormy weather; however, the gale is hushed to a calm. As there is a good carpenter, a wheelwright and a ship's carpenter on board they all set to work making a new jibboom for the vessel, and John Fulford is making a ladder for the hatchway.'

The crew would also on occasion do something to lessen the passengers' boredom. W. Gliddon wrote on board the *Ocean Queen*:

'The crew leave work at 6 p.m. after which they amuse themselves and us, as they please. This evening they made their appearance on deck equipped as soldiers: they were capitally made-up; instead of a drum they had a tin box, and this greatly aided the burlesque. They marched aft to the cabin and one of the "ossifers" handed the Captain a letter, the purport was that there was reason to suspect that one of their recruits was on board and that if he detained him any longer, he would have to take the consequences. The Captain gave them liberty to search the ship, and take him if they found him, which of course they very soon did; by this time two others of the crew had made their appearance equipped as countrymen. After some parleying of course they were enlisted and marched off to learn their exercise; not liking drill very well they ran away, and one was concealed in the long-boat, and when questioned as to the cause of his running off he answered that he "ware towld to vall back, and he valled into the boat". The other's excuse was that he "went to see the maester he was gwine to live wi', when they 'listed en, but when we got the gate, he seed his *apprehension*, and he wur frightened". This is only a specimen of the wit and humour displayed by the crew and I do not think any ship possesses a better crew.'

Not all wooden sailing ships went on long voyages. Perhaps the bulk of passengers in number through most of the nineteenth century made short passages across the English Channel or the North Sea in packet ships sailing at more or less scheduled times. On these relatively short journeys many people remained on deck throughout the voyage. Those who bought berths did so in communal accommodation, men and women lying in curtained bunks built into the side of a central cabin where food was served while those around were often wretched with sea sickness. These conditions of travel which were a widely shared experience, were the subject of contemporary humorous illustrations, concentrating always on the fears and miseries of the passage rather than on its delights.

The concept of the ocean-going packet ship running to schedule, the precursor of the liner on long voyages on deep water, was a product of early nineteenth century North American thinking. It began with the Black Ball Line sailing between New York and Liverpool in 1818. The ships of this line differed from all their contemporaries in that they sailed on a fixed day of the month from a determined port – New York or Liverpool – regardless of the cargo loaded or the number of passengers booked. All their contemporaries waited until they had a reasonable quota of both. To sail on a fixed date intent on making a fast passage was so great an advantage to both shippers and travellers that the service prospered and in the 1820s became well-established with rival firms in the field. In 1822 the Black Ball Line instituted fortnightly sailings on the 1st and 16th of the month. They set up an average of twenty-three days for the eastwards Atlantic crossing, forty days to the westward and the cost of travelling in this preferred service with a certain departure date and a reasonable average voyage was very high, thirty-five guineas for the cabin passenger, so the majority of passengers continued to travel by the old wandering unscheduled merchant ships.

By the middle of the century the expensive accommodation of the packet was quite different from that provided by an ordinary merchant ship. A few contemporary sketches painted in 1851 show scenes below decks in the *Margaret Evans*, built in 1846 for the American Black X Line which had vessels sailing on 1st of each month for London from New York and from London for New York. The *Margaret Evans* was of 900 tons – the largest vessel the line had owned to this date. The cabin passengers enjoyed the run of the stern cabin with its great windows and the traditional sofa across the whole breadth of the stern. Forward the long saloon was amidships, between the doors of the staterooms lining the sides of the vessel, under the poop deck. Down the greater part of the length of the saloon ran a long table with benches on either side. The staterooms were relatively comfortable with wooden washstands with pitchers of water and washbowls let into circular holes in the stand top so that they would not slide about with the vessel's motion. A padded bench had drawers under it secured with wooden turnbuckles so that they would not fly open when the vessel rolled. There was a chair and two bunks, one above the other, with curtains. The floor was carpeted. These were as comfortable quarters as had ever been provided at sea for any but the very rich and it is to be noted that the furniture, simple as it was, was provided as part of the ship's equipment and not by the passenger. The ship was permanently equipped for passengers. Sea travel had come of age. It was at last not normally a once-and-for-all adventure, involving the moving of house and home, but something done by passengers requiring the convenience of fully furnished accommodation.

At the same period, the early 1850s, a similar change took place in the type of accommodation offered in the vessels employed in the Australian trade. The discovery of the gold fields created a big demand both for transport and for better quality accommodation. One of the vessels which provided jt, the *James Baines*, built in the United States to the order of British shipowners for this new market was described by a contemporary newspaper as follows:

'She has full topgallant foc's'le, which extends to the foremast and is fitted for the accommodation of her crew; and abaft the foremast a large house, which contains spacious galleys, several staterooms, storerooms, an ice room and shelters a staircase which leads to the decks below. She has a full poop deck, between seven and eight feet high, under which is the cabin for female passengers and before it a large house which contains the dining saloon and other apartments . . . Besides these the cabin contains eleven spacious staterooms, a bathroom and other useful apartments.

'The dining saloon is thirty-five feet long by fifteen feet wide; the entrance to the deck from the saloon is two and a half feet wide . . . and opposite the midship door of the saloon is the pantry, which is spacious and fitted up in superior style. In front of the saloon house are the staterooms of the First and Second officers, and the windows of these rooms are of stained glass and have the ship's name in them. The staircase in the after part of the saloon leads to the main deck, where are the gentlemen's sleeping apartments, twenty-four in all, each stateroom having two berths. . . . The lower decks are ventilated amidships with trunked skylights which pass through the house forward as well as the cabin saloon aft. The height between each of the decks is seven and a half feet.'

'Boston Atlas', 1854, Quoted in Basil Lubbock, 'The Colonial Clippers', Glasgow, 1921

So even the 'tween decks passengers had considerably more than standing room. A contemporary vessel, the *Marco Polo*, bought out of the Canadian timber trade and converted to passenger-carrying, was equipped even better. The *Illustrated London News* in 1852 wrote of her as follows;

'The *Marco Polo* is a three-decker, and having been built expressly for the passenger trade (sic) is nothing short in capacity or equipment. Her height between decks is eight feet, and no pains have been spared in her construction to secure through ventilation. . . .

'On deck forward of the poop, which is used as a ladies' cabin, is a "home on deck" to be used as a dining saloon. It is ceiled with maple and the pilasters are panelled with richly ornamented and silvered glass – coins of various countries being a novel feature of the decorations. Between each pilaster is a circular aperture about 6 feet in circumference for light and ventilation; over it is placed a sheet of plate glass with a cleverly painted picturesque view in the centre with a frame work of foliage and scroll in opaque colours and gold. The whole panels are brought

22

out slightly by the rim of perforated zinc, so that not only does light from the ventilator diffuse itself over the whole but air is freely admitted.

'The saloon doors are panelled in stained glass bearing figures of commerce and industry from the designs of Mr Frank Howard. In the centre of the saloon is a table or dumb-waiter made of thick plate glass, which has the advantage of giving light to the dormitories below. The upholstery is in embossed crimson velvet.

'The berths in separate staterooms are ranged in the 'tween decks and are rendered cheerful by circular glass hatch-lights of novel and effective construction.'

By the time the sailing passenger-carrying vessel had reached these levels it was already under the critical threat of the steamer and although the process was not a simple nor a smooth one, the fast steamer was eventually to become the pace-setter in passenger accommodation at sea. By 1860 the wooden sailing vessel had given way to steam in the passenger trade on the North Atlantic and she was then soon to give place to iron and steel sailing vessels on the long run to Australasia. Nine years later the Suez Canal opened the Indian passenger trade to steam-powered vessels.

During the whole of the era of the wooden sailing ship masters and mates shared accommodation with cabin passengers when they were carried and lived in comparable conditions when they were not. Even in the smallest vessels the accommodation was often very comfortable by the standards of the society in which the ships' officers lived. The accommodation of the very small wooden bark *Pride of Wales*, in the 1890s, for instance, was described by a working passenger, Henry Hughes, as follows:

'The cabin was cosy. It had mahogany panels with a white ceiling, and a decorative skylight in which hung a tell-tale compass and a swing paraffin lamp and the usual barometer and clock. Leather settees surrounded a mahogany table. There was a snug copper fireplace with a mirror above the mantlepiece. The captain's berth led out on the starboard side. There was an after cabin which was dark and dingy, lighted only by deadlights. The chief mate's berth led in one direction on the port side, and that of the boatswain and mine on the other. The only light that penetrated these bunks struggled through a small deck deadlight. I could not see the foot of my bed except by the aid of artificial light. Lots of things I had lost used to find their way there.'

Henry Hughes, 'Through Mighty Seas', London, not dated

The accommodation of the crews of the vessels compared with that provided in the 'tween decks for the emigrants. Situated right in the bows of the ship, invariably below the deck, the 'forecastle' of a wooden sailing vessel of the first eighty years of the nineteenth century was a dark, usually damp space containing little but the bunks in which the men slept, space for the stowing of sea chests and a table at which they ate. It was entered by means of the forecastle scuttle and a steeply sloping ladder. It was heated by a stove with a funnel pipe rising through the deck and covered with a cowl at the top to keep out some of the water. In good ships there were candles and oil lamps. In bad ones the crew had to make their own light by rendering down fat from the food and using cotton wool as a wick in an old tin. Sometimes there was not even a table and the crew had to eat their food sitting on the floor, sanitary arrangements comprised nothing except a wooden shelter on deck and sometimes only wooden buckets.

In the first half of the century many vessels did not provide even bunks for the men who, in naval style, were expected to bring their own hammocks. In small merchant ships the use of hammocks persisted until late in the century. The trading ketch *Hobah* built in 1879, which one of the authors knew very well in childhood, was not fitted with bunks until just before World War I. In old ships some men actually preferred hammocks because they could rig an oil skin on a line above them as a fly sheet to keep off the drips from leaking decks above.

In 1834 a vessel of 420 tons, flush-decked and with three masts, which must have looked very like the ship in Plate 9, had only one deckhouse, the galley where the food was cooked. All the rest of the accommodation for the crew of 21 was below decks. The master, two mates and the steward lived in the stern cabin aft, the carpenter cooper and one apprentice in a square space boarded off from the cargo in the after hatch. The cook, ten seamen and three apprentices lived in a below deck forecastle, 20 feet long by 5 feet high. There was a small scuttle entrance, no lighting or ventilation, hammocks and no tables or seats. The men's sea chests were the only furniture.

For long after they had ceased to be used as passenger-carriers wooden sailing ships continued to be built for cargo alone. The last to be constructed in England were launched just before World War I, but in the United States and Canada great wooden vessels carrying many thousands of tons of cargo were built until the 1920s and in Scandinavia smaller wooden sailing vessels continued to be launched until the middle of the century.

In these later wooden vessels, conditions for the crews were very different from those of the 1850s, often the accommodation was in a deck house in the neighbourhood of the foremast with a separate compartment for the galley where the food was cooked so that, served through a sliding hatch, it reached the fo'c'sle table still hot. In some big American vessels the fo'c'sle was centrally heated using steam from the boiler to the donkey engines. Although in no way comparing with the accommodation provided for seamen today, these later wooden sailing vessels had living quarters as good or better than that of steamships of the same period. Some old ships were similarly converted. The *Pride of Wales*, built at Portmadoc in 1868, was refitted in 1890 and a new forecastle and galley built on deck abaft the foremast to replace the squalid quarters below the windlass where the crew had previously lived. The famous ship *Cutty Sark* was similarly treated during her long career as a merchant vessel.

The accommodation for the crews of wooden sailing fishing vessels was even simpler than that of the smaller merchant ships. The same general plan of central table, bunks built into the side of the vessel, and lockers, was used but the deckhead was lower and the amount of cubic space available for each man even less. This was a spartan existence indeed, though better than that in the worst of the emigrant vessels of the 1840s.

CHAPTER THREE

Iron and Steel Sailing Ships as Passenger Carriers

The end of the wooden sailing ship as a passenger carrier came suddenly, almost dramatically, in the 1860s. In the North Atlantic trade she gave way to the steamer. For some years this process had been going on gradually as the packet trade for cabin passengers shifted over to power-driven vessels, but for the bulk of passengers, the emigrants, the wooden sailing vessel with all the discomforts of the six week average westerly passage remained the normal means of transport right through the 1850s. There were a number of reasons for this, but the most important single factor was the cheapness of the accommodation offered. Vessels in the timber trade from Canada could never find sufficient outward cargo so that the fares of passengers, even when they were fixed at little above the cost of providing food and service, represented a net return where there would otherwise have been none.

But the change when it did come, came very quickly. Thus in 1858, 138 sailing ships carried over 9,000 steerage passengers from Britain to Quebec – the greatest single port of immigration into North America. There were only 19 steamers in the trade which carried less than 2,000 passengers. But only two years later, 37 steamers carried almost 7,000 passengers, 20 sailing vessels less than 1,000. The day of the wooden sailing vessel as a passenger carrier on a large scale on the North Atlantic was over.

Nothing so dramatic took place on the long haul to Australasia. By 1852 steam-and-sail vessels like the *Calcutta* and the famous *Great Britain* were offering excellent accommodation by the standards of the times, but despite the advantage of the relatively predictable passages of the steam assisted vessels and the very much higher standards of accommodation they offered, wooden sailing vessels remained predominant in this long range trade until the 1860s. A good turning point might be taken as the sale of the first White Star Line in 1867. It had been formed to run fine wooden ships to Australia after the gold discoveries of the early 1850s and its vessels had included such contemporarily famous ships as the *Red Jacket*, one of the best known clippers of her day. The successor to the Line's founders purchased iron sailing vessels for the same trade and ran them under the same White Star flag.

The iron and steel sailing ship as a passenger carrier was a phenomenon of the Australian trade. Elsewhere in the world the steamer had become the normal vehicle for the movement of human beings at sea, though sailing vessels, even wooden ones, continued to carry cargoes in different parts of the world until the middle of the twentieth century. There were a number of reasons why the metal sailing vessel served as a passenger carrier to Australia and New Zealand. The most important was probably that the trade offered peculiar advantages to sailing ships and therefore the vessels tended to be prosperously run and to offer good accommodation at relatively low prices. And of course there were people to be moved, emigrants of all classes by their tens of thousands to these countries as their populations rapidly expanded in the 1860s and 70s.

The trade was profitable because it could be geared to Australian harvests of wool and of wheat and linked with the Indian trade in jute and rice. Because the outward cargoes offering were limited it paid to give attention to passenger carrying and because the distance sailed on each voyage was so vast and the trade based on a single outward and a single homeward cargo the powered vessel had fewer advantages than in most businesses. Because this was a trade in which sails could compete with steam the passenger tradition lingered on. Even in the early twentieth century a few great steel sailing vessels were regularly offering passages to Australia, the last opportunity men and women will ever have to travel across the ocean under sail in regular merchant vessels built and fitted out as passenger carriers.

One of the first iron sailing vessels in the Australian trade was in fact a pioneer steamer, the *Calcutta*, which after her steaming days were over was converted into a full rigged ship – square-rigged on all her three masts – and re-named *Darling Downs*. Under that name she was a very popular vessel with passengers between London and Sydney. Great efforts were made to provide passenger accommodation in these iron vessels which would meet the standards set by the best of the wooden packet ships and clippers and greatly improved upon by the steamers of the 60s. Thus when the *Loch Maree* was built in 1873 she was given first-class accommodation, arranged on the lines of contemporary Peninsular and Oriental Company steamers (see Chapter Six) under a poop deck over fifty feet long.

A contemporary of the *Loch Maree* was the *Rodney* and there survives a detailed description of her accommodation as it appeared to an Australian journalist in 1874 and which reveals by what it praises how crude the normal accommodation of the period still was:

'She has been constructed specially with a view to the conveyance of passengers, and there are few sailing ships coming to the Colony which have such a spacious saloon. It measures 80 feet in length and has berthing accommodation for sixty people . . . the cabins are 10 feet square, and a number of the sleeping berths can be drawn out so as to accommodate two people. For each cabin there is a fixed lavatory, [washbowl], supplied with fresh water from a patent tap, and by the removal of a small plug in the centre of the basin, the water runs right away into the sea, so that all slopping is avoided. The lavatory is fixed on top of a cupboard, which answers all the purposes of a little chiffoniere, being fitted up for the reception of bottles, glasses, brushes, etc.

'There is also a chest of drawers in each cabin – a very great convenience – in which may be kept clothes, books, linen and many "unconsidered trifles", which generally go knocking about in ship's cabins at sea.

'The windows in the cabins are large, admitting plenty of light and air, and the passengers have easy control over them . . . Good sized looking glasses and handy little racks for water bottles, tumblers, combs, brushes, etc., also abound, and in other little matters the comfort of the passengers has been well cared for.

26

'The cabins are also so arranged that two or more or even the whole of them on one side of the ship afford communication to each other without going out into the saloon, and where families are together this is very advantageous.

'The bathroom occupies the space of one of the largest cabins, and hot as well as cold baths are attainable.'

Quoted in Basil Lubbock, 'The Colonial Clippers', Glasgow, 1921.

The *Rodney* was competing for passengers against the early Orient liners and other steam vessels which, equipped with efficient and economical compound engines were making the voyage to Sydney in fifty days. The best of sailing ships on a very good passage took sixty-five to seventy-five days. Many passages were of ninety days or often more than one hundred days. But these passages were shorter than those of wooden sailing ships twenty years before and the accommodation was incomparably better. It was all a long way from the *Charlotte Jane,* even further from an emigrant deck of the 1840s.

And not only the Australian emigrant business gave rise to iron sailing ships with a high standard of passenger accommodation. The New Zealand emigrant trade developed in the early 1870s and gave rise to a class of fast iron passenger-carrying sailing ships, smaller than many of their contemporaries but larger than the *Charlotte Jane*. In the spring of 1874 alone 3,000 emigrants left Britain for New Zealand on board vessels of this type built for the New Zealand Shipping Company which sent nearly 30,000 emigrants to the colony in three years. Ten years later, in 1884, a young woman whom we know only as 'Hannah' made a passage to New Zealand in the iron full-rigged ship *Zealandia,* built in 1869, of just over 1,000 tons and operated by the firm of Shaw, Saville and Albion. The vessel was about the same size as the *Cutty Sark*, which now lies in her dry dock at Greenwich, but was constructed entirely of iron instead of being planked in wood. She was considered at the time to be well-fitted out for passengers with unusually large and well ventilated cabins. She had first, second and third class accommodation. Hannah travelled second class with her sister Ruth and they had accommodation in a cabin in a deck house.

The feeding arrangements for the second and third class passengers as described in an introduction to Hannah's journal, of which there is a copy in the National Maritime Museum, were interesting:

'The 'tween decks were fitted so that mess tables could be hoisted up to the deck above when they were not in use, thus giving as much space as possible in the evenings when the deck above was not available. All well regulated ships arranged that each mess had a mess captain who maintained the discipline in his little section, drew the stores, supervised the preparation of food for the galleys and did all that was necessary to prevent things from getting into such a state that they had to be brought to the Captain's notice. . . . The livestock which was shipped on deck was principally for the use of saloon passengers, but as much as possible would find its way into the 'tween decks, whose passengers otherwise had to live on salt beef, barrelled pork, tinned mutton and highly smoked bacon, with preserved potatoes, carrots, etc., and hard biscuits more often than not. Lime juice was served out to the

27

emigrants in the same way as it was to the seamen under the Merchant Shipping Act. The principal sweets were rice and sago puddings, which were apt to become monotonous, the special ''duffs'' not being quite the delicacy that they were labelled when they had to be made with salt water.'

These customs are reflected in Hannah's journal which is in places very revealing of conditions of sea travel quite removed from those of the late twentieth century, even though she travelled less than a hundred years ago in what was considered to be a crack vessel. The passengers in the second class did some of their own cooking – and their cabins were very sparsely furnished so that, like the sea travellers of an earlier age, they brought some of their own equipment with them. Hannah wrote:

Sunday 20th

'After a rough and sleepless night I was aroused at 5 a.m. by one of our gentlemen asking for our water can. We put the can out and turn over with the intention of having a little sleep. But at 6.30 there was a general babble to know what we would like for breakfast, which was a sign that they were getting over their seasickness. We decided to have some ham, then there was a consultation how it was to be cooked. We found it was no use trying to sleep, so we turned out and had our breakfast. After which it was time to think about dinner, for we were all finding our appetites. I and Ruth take some plums on deck to stone. Mrs B makes a pudding which we all enjoy for dinner. Afternoon on deck reading and singing. We have travelled 147 miles since 12 a.m. yesterday. . . .'

Monday 21st

'. . . Breakfast at 8.30 of grilled ham and kippered herrings. After which I help steward to wash up with a view of showing him the best way. He is awkward at it, being quite new work to him. He is a compositor working his way out. He is thankful for the few hints we give him! . . .'

Tuesday 22nd

'Aroused at 5 a.m. by a great rattling of crockery etc and the gentlemen getting our water for us. We are feeling very sick again. We have had a dreadful tossing all night, and the water has come in our porthole and wetted Miss A's bed. We dress this morning with great difficulty being dashed from one side of the cabin to the other. Miss A is ready first, she walks out on deck, thinking of blowing her sick headache away. The minute she steps out the sea rushes over and drenches her. She comes in looking so pitiful, and finds during her absence her hood has fallen from its hook into a basin of water. . . .'

Thursday 24th

'. . . It is much warmer and we are sitting on deck at work and the sheep are walking about. They are getting so tame they come and put their noses in our laps and rub about us like a pet dog. We shall feel it cruel to eat them when the time comes for them to be killed. . . .'

Thursday May 1st

'. . . It seems too hot to turn in our berths tonight, combined with a fear of the rats running over us. I volunteer to stay in the saloon and keep watch, time Ruth and Miss A sleep. I took my pillow and sat down in the saloon with my head on the table and my eyes fixed on the partition where the rats come over. But I could not rest a minute, there always seems to be somebody on board ship ready for mischief. The officer on watch on the poop began dropping paper down upon me through the skylight. I found there would be no peace for me there so I turned in my bunk at 12.30. Ruth and Miss A appeared to be asleep and all was quiet for about half an hour. I was just dozing off when Ruth startled me by jumping out quickly and knocking several things down and kicking against my bunk on her way. I was soon up and striking a light to see what it meant. I found one of our usual visitors had made his appearance on top of the partition and leaped down on her face. The ship was then rolling and pitching very much. Three of our gentlemen heard the noise and guessing the cause thought they would come and try to catch the intruder. As they were hurrying towards us, a sudden lurch of the ship threw them down with a bang against our cabin door, which startled us almost as much as the rat. But they soon righted themselves, and asked admittance when the search was commenced. The horrid little creature was found comfortably lying under Ruth's pillow. He made a rush when he was discovered, and ran along the top of the partition, Mr. M gave him two good crumps but I fear was not successful in hurting him much. It was a long time before we had courage to turn in again for fear there might still be one lurking in the corner. We sat there until daybreak when sleep gained the mastery. We were just lost at 6 a.m. when the first mate came and called out whales to be seen, but we were too tired to feel interested in whales or any other monster.'

The masters and mates of these steel sailing ships were comfortably housed in accommodation often reminiscent of middle class houses ashore and furnished with items which in general might have been used in these houses in the suburbs of London or Liverpool or Glasgow. Their accommodation was under the poop, or in the after end of a midships house, often at the end of the century built right across the vessel as part of her main structure. The crews of such vessels lived in the fore end of the midships house in conditions of relative comfort. Others lived in deckhouse forecastles like those built into the later wooden sailing ships. But in many ships, right down to the last days of sail, crews still existed in the 'topgallant fo'c's'le' right in the bows of the vessel, which was unheated and unprotected against the sea and shared with the windlass and the end of the chain cable. Such a forecastle, where twenty men might live with no private space except their own bunks, is graphically described in Conrad's *The Nigger of the Narcissus*.

PART TWO
THE STEAMSHIP

CHAPTER FOUR

The Accommodation in Early Steamers

The steamship, first developed in the early years of the nineteenth century, was a very long time coming to fruition as a vehicle for ocean transport in competition with the sailing ship in all the trades of the world. It was not until the 1860s and the development of an efficient and economical compound engine and its successful application at sea by the Ocean Steamship Company that the steamer was finally demonstrated to be potentially the normal vehicle for general overseas trade. The ways of industry and commerce took a while to become adopted to the new means of sea transport, but from those years onwards, for all the tremendous developments which were still to take place in the design and building of sailing ships and which resulted in the development of the steel four-masted bark in Britain and of the five- and six-masted wooden schooners in the United States, their days were predictably numbered.

In the first half of the nineteenth century it was therefore on short sea routes and with valuable cargoes that the early, generally uneconomical, steamers first established themselves. We have described and illustrated the discomforts of the sailing vessel in all its forms as a vehicle for passengers. It was by modern standards most uncomfortable even in its final form, the great iron or steel vessel of two or three thousand tons, like the *Falls of Clyde,* It is not surprising, therefore, that it was as passenger vessels on rivers and on short sea routes around the coasts of Britain and the United States that steamers first became accepted as profitable earning units of the merchant shipping industry. Here the disadvantages from which they suffered, engines which absorbed vast quantities of coal in relation to the power developed and distance steamed, the inefficiency of the paddle as a propelling device and its unsuitability for use in rough water, and the sheer difficulty of carrying enough fuel, mattered least. The fact that they could offer fast, regular and relatively reliable service meant they could compete with the uncomfortable and irregular sailing packets, even though their fares had to be high.

In the United States the development of the steamboat had a particular source of impetus – the commercial navigation of the Mississippi and other rivers and the opening up of the vast surrounding territories, the provision of regular services on the Hudson and other major arteries of communication in a rapidly developing economy. In Canada there was a similar factor, if commercially on a smaller scale, in the provision of regular communications up the St Lawrence from Quebec, and on the Great Lakes. Indeed, the history of the commercial steamship really begins after a century of experiments in Britain and Europe with the successful operation in regular service on the Hudson for seven years from 1808 of the *North River Steamboat of Clermont,* using a single cylinder engine built by the British firm of Boulton and Watt. She was the product of the genius and drive of Robert Fulton and she was rapidly followed by a number of other vessels of his design including the first steam warship, the *Demologos,* designed to fight for the United States in the War of 1812 but not completed in time to do so. By 1817 the *Chancellor Livingstone,* launched after Fulton's death, was steaming from Albany to New York in eighteen hours, carrying 120 passengers with berths and many more deck passengers.

The *North River Steamboat of Clermont* was an expensive vehicle to travel in. It cost $7 to steam all the way from New York City to Albany and each meal cost 50 cents. But children under five could travel half price, providing they slept two in a berth. Servants were carried for two-thirds fare if they occupied a berth, one half fare if they travelled on deck. Every passenger who paid the full fare was allowed sixty pounds of baggage (which, it is to be noted, is roughly the same as the free baggage allowance currently in force for first class international air passengers) and they had to pay at 3 cents per pound for excess baggage. The less than full fare baggage allowance was close to the normal tourist air travel baggage allowance of today, that is it was forty pounds. A contemporary advertisement explains the system of feeding passengers:

'Passengers will breakfast before they come aboard. Dinner will be served up exactly at 1 o'clock; tea, with meats, which is also supper at 8 o'clock in the evening; and breakfast at 9 o'clock in the morning. No one has a claim on the steward for victuals at any other time.'

The early development of the American steamboat was assisted by two other factors—the fact that the United States was not embroiled in the European wars of Napoleon and the existence of vast quantities of virtually free fuel in the forests on the banks of the rivers on which the steamboats plied. The *Chancellor Livingstone* burned coal, but almost all her contemporaries and many of her successors for nearly a century burned wood. Fulton foresaw the great importance that the steamboat was to have in the opening up of the West. On his return to New York from the first voyage of the *North River Steamboat of Clermont* he wrote to a friend:

'. . . it will give a quick and cheap conveyance to the merchandise on the Mississippi, Missouri, and other great rivers, which are now laying open their treasures to the enterprise of our countrymen; . . .'

In 1811 the first steamboat to ply on the western rivers, the *New Orleans,* was built in Pittsburg. She had two cabins, one forward and one aft. The after cabin, containing only four berths, was for females, the larger and better placed forward cabin was for men. The successful pioneering journeys of this vessel led to the construction in 1813 of the *Vesuvius,* a paddle steamer over 150 feet long, built by Robert Fulton, again at Pittsburg. Her sixty-foot-long main cabin contained about sixty berths and below the main deck was a ladies' cabin. In 1814 she was placed in service between Louisville and New Orleans and thus began the steamboat's important contribution to the establishment of the modern United States.

By 1833 there were 300 steamboats employed on the inland waterways and the coastal trade of the United States. Between 1830 and 1850 the total of steam tonnage in United States river trade was greater than the total steam tonnage registered as British. The steamboat especially on the Mississippi, partly as a result of the work of Mark

Twain, forms part of the modern image of the American way of life of the middle of the nineteenth century and these steamboats and also those in the coastal passenger trade of New England, and in service on Lake Champlain, are for many people part of the American mythology of today. American steamboats established a tradition of passenger comfort, almost of luxury, at an early stage. Their accommodation was based from earliest years on a long, high, narrow central saloon which occupied most of the length of the vessel.

Steamboats in North America retained this central compartment until far into the century, as they retained also an early established tradition of baroque opulence, over-decorated and sumptuous in their public apartments. Sometimes, later in the century, passengers were to be entertained with steam organs, always there were great areas of carved woodwork and frosted glass. There was an added entertainment for passengers too. Under the influence of the successful early Boulton and Watt beam engines imported into North America United States engineers continued to prefer this class of machinery, not only for river craft but also for vessels on short sea routes, long after beam engines had been abandoned in Britain in favour, at first, of the more compact side-lever engines (the only surviving pair of which can be seen in full operation in the National Maritime Museum's paddle tug *Reliant*) and later of the diagonal engine used in pleasure paddle steamers in the early years of this century. The accommodation of many American steamboats was so arranged that it was possible to view the great 'walking beams' going steadily up and down for hour after hour with their massive twelve foot strokes. These engines were reliable, economical, easy to maintain and relatively simple to build. Many of them outlasted two or even three hulls and the walking beam was one of the characteristics of American steamers until well into the present century.

The steamboats soon moved off the rivers into the open sea. By March 1815 the *Fulton* steamed along Long Island Sound from New York to New Haven and in 1817 the *Fire Fly* started a service between Newport and Providence. In 1828, the *Chancellor Livingstone* herself was moved on to the Sound service. In her early days on this line it was the custom for the stewards to place decanters of brandy and other spirits on the table for the passengers to help themselves. In 1829 this pleasant custom ceased, wine was substituted and there was a public outcry. The directors defended themselves by pointing out that spirits could still be purchased from the bars. In the same year as this little rumpus the first steamer to have separate staterooms, the *President*, entered service in Long Island Sound. Soon steam vessels were running the length of the coast of New England. They could offer far better service than the sailing packets and at competitive rates, so on the whole they prospered.

The St Lawrence is the main natural highway of Eastern Canada. Its ascent has always been an arduous process for sailing and rowing craft. It is not surprising therefore that Canadian enterprise followed very closely on that of the United States and by 1809, three years before Bell's *Comet* inaugurated European steamship services by steaming on the Clyde, a service was established between Quebec and Montreal with the steamer *Accommodation*. In the words of a contemporary press account:

'She has at present berths for twenty passengers, which next year will be considerably augmented. No wind or tide can stop her. The price for a passage up is $9 and $8 down – the vessel supplying the provisions.'

There survive descriptions of the accommodation in some of these early river and coastal steam vessels of eastern North America. The *Royal William*, built for service in the Gulf of St Lawrence and still sometimes wrongly described as the first vessel to have steamed across the North Atlantic, was reported in a Canadian newspaper in 1831 in the following terms:

'Her under deck cabin is fitted up with upwards of fifty ample berths and a large parlour. In a round house on deck is a spacious dining room. The whole of the cabin is fitted up with elegance and taste of the best style.'

Another contemporary was even more enthusiastic:

'Her accommodations for passengers are of the first description. Her cabins are elegant, and the sleeping berths, of which there are about 50, admirable. The round house contains a spacious dining room, handsomely fitted up, capable of accommodating 100 persons. The steerage is also roomy and comfortable and there is ample space on deck . . . The engines, which are of 180 horsepower, are certainly highly finished, and finely polished; her rate of sailing we have not learnt. But her engines are of excellent construction, we should think them capable of propelling her with ease and comfort at a rate of at least 10 miles an hour.'

A few years later the steamer *Rose* which had been bought in England to establish a service across the Northumberland Strait between Nova Scotia and Prince Edward Island was being described in glowing terms:

'This vessel . . . is intended to run between this port [Charlottetown] and Pictou, for the purpose of covering the mail, passengers, etc. The *Rose* has excellent accommodation for passengers, her principal cabin being sufficiently large to seat comfortably three dozen persons. The cabin for lady passengers is also very convenient . . . This vessel is now fitted up in first rate style – everything that can tend to the comfort and convenience of passengers has been bestowed on her; and, commanded by an experienced and obliging Master, we can confidently assert that travellers will find on board all that can render the voyage speedy and pleasant.'

In Britain something of a boom in steamship building took place in the 1820s. After the close of the Napoleonic Wars, with the rapid development of the Industrial Revolution numerous engine-building companies were set up. Iron became cheaper and more readily available and new machine tools made its working easier and new processes possible. Steamboats could be built in many yards and they were, but none on the scale of the Canadian and American enterprises of the same period. Nevertheless, the advantages of the steamer over the sailing packet in river, estuary and short sea trade were proved and obvious. After the technical success of Bell's *Comet* of 1812, paddle steamers began rapidly to appear on a number of routes. By the end of the Napoleonic Wars in 1815 there were thirteen steamers operating on the Clyde, twenty-six more by 1819 and by 1830 a total of seventy-one steamers had been built on the Clyde and were steaming up the west coast as far as Skye, as well as in the several other parts of the world to which some of them had laboriously made their way.

For these 100-foot wooden paddle steamers, driven by early forms of side-lever engine and equipped with tall thin funnels and masts and sails, were successful not only in Scottish waters. By mid-1815 a steamer had steamed from the Clyde to Liverpool. It is characteristic of the casualness of public attention towards these early steam vessels, which makes the detailed recording of their history very difficult, that her name is not known, but the *Liverpool Mercury* reported that 'we believe she is intended to ply between this port and Runcorn, or even occasionally as far as Warrington. Her cabin will contain about 100 passengers'. A year later a regular service across the Irish sea was started to and from Holyhead. In 1815 also, a momentous year in the history of the development of the British steamship, the *Marjory* steamed from the Clyde to the Thames, being as far as is known the first vessel ever to do so. She travelled through the Forth and Clyde Canal and down the east coast, and then established the first steamer service on the Thames, from London to Margate. Here she was rapidly joined by other vessels, including the *Thames* ex *Argyle*, which, under Captain George Dodd, steamed to London from the Clyde in an historic passage via the Irish Sea, Dublin, a rounding of Land's End and the running of the length of the English Channel.

This passage is of particular interest because the *Thames* carried two passengers from Dublin to London, a Mr and Mrs Weld, and Mrs Weld was certainly the first woman to make an open sea voyage in a British steamer. Mr Weld kept a journal of the passage which was subsequently published:

'On the 25th May, 1815, I heard by accident that a steam-vessel had arrived at Dublin. I immediately went to see her, and found her on the point of starting with a number of curious visitors upon an experimental trip in the bay. I was so much pleased with all that I saw and heard concerning her, that, having previously intended to proceed to London, I determined to request Captain Dodd to receive me as a passenger, and to be permitted to accompany him throughout the voyage. He at once consented, and my wife having resolved on sharing the dangers of the voyage with me, we proceeded to make the necessary arrangements for our departure. On the 28th of May, being Sunday, we left the Liffey at noon. Many persons embarked with us from curiosity, but only to cross the bay as far as Dunleary (now Kingstown), where they landed. Unfortunately, the sea was very rough, which occasioned the most violent sea-sickness amongst the passengers. . . .

'The sea was comparatively calm as the vessel steamed into the Bay of Dalkey, and the passengers calculated on a pleasant voyage during the night, but, when beyond the shelter of the coast, they found it to be as rough as ever. The *Thames* again proved her admirable sea-going qualities, bounding so lightly over the waves that her passengers were not once wetted, even by the spray.'

Quoted in 'The History of Steam Navigation', by John Kennedy, Liverpool, 1903

They had a successful voyage, in the course of which the *Thames* behaved very well indeed, steaming all the way and attracting great attention wherever she put in. She was eighty feet long and her paddle wheels were nine feet in diameter. Her tall funnel did duty as a mast and a square sail could be set from it, like that in the steamship on the right-hand side of Plate 40. She had galleries not only in the stern, like a sailing ship, but also all the length of her, broken only by the paddle boxes, so that she looked much longer than she really was. The main passenger deck was on the level of this gallery and the cabin windows opened on to it. When she had settled down on her London to Margate service she was described in interesting terms in *The Times*:

'Her cabins are spacious, and are fitted up with all that elegance could suggest, or personal comfort require; presenting a choice library, backgammon boards, draught tables, and other means of amusement. For the express purpose of combining delicacy with comfort a female servant attends upon the ladies. The fares (which include Pier Duty) are in the Chief Cabin 15s, and in the Fore Cabin 11s, children half price. No articles or goods will be taken, except the luggage accompanying passengers; and the proprietors will not be answerable for any of the above, unless delivered into the care of the Steward, nor to the amount of more than £5 value, except entered and paid for as such.'

By 1817 steam vessels were being built on the Tyne and it is through one of these that we get the very first glimpse of the accommodation in a British steamship, (Plate 41). By 1818 there were six steamships registered as of the Port of London. One of these was the *Victory*, built at Rotherhithe under the supervision of Captain George Dodd, Master of the *Thames* on her historic voyage, for a service between Richmond and Margate. Through this vessel we get a second view of the accommodation in one of these early British steam packets. An engraving of the *Victory*, (Plate 42) published in 1821 in London, is embellished by two insets showing her accommodation fore and aft. She had an all-round gallery with windows down her length on either side like the *Thames*. The long cabins are furnished with side benches which are the main seating place of the passengers and with only a little furniture in the main body of the cabin. The cabin walls are panelled, the ceilings moulded. The four stern windows copied from the contemporary sailing ships are very obvious in the view of the after cabin. If these drawings represent the reality, passengers between London and Margate in 1818 could rely on travelling in conditions almost of luxury. The fares, of course, were expensive. The 15s (75p) for the after cabin represented two weeks' wages for a labouring man, and it is not surprising that the passengers in the engraving of the *Victory* appear elegantly dressed, as can be seen in the reproductions at the end of this chapter (Plates 43 and 44).

The second class cabin is not illustrated. This was much less luxurious accommodation and in a contemporary of the *Victory* on the same run, the *London Engineer* it is reported that the hard seats and cramped conditions in the second class accommodation contrasted badly with the spacious saloon aft.

In 1819 a regular service was established between Liverpool and Belfast with the *Waterloo*, owned by a firm which also operated a fleet of sailing packets between the two ports. The contrast must have been obvious and illustrates the reasons for the rapid expansion of the steam packet services. In the smacks the duration of the passage and therefore the date and hour of sailing were totally unpredictable. The accommodation cannot have been very much better than that illustrated in Plate 17, and the journey would be wet, cold and very uncomfortable. In the *Waterloo* there was a dining room capable of taking all the cabin passengers at one sitting, 'a separate and neatly decorated cabin for ladies and ten state rooms which could be hired by families. There were berths for twenty-two cabin passengers and steerage passengers could cross for 10s 6d (52$\frac{1}{2}$p) in twenty-four hours and sail any Monday or Friday from Liverpool.

We have already remarked on the comparatively little public attention these early steamships attracted. At the beginning of a new era in transport the pioneers were lucky if they got a passing mention in the local press. Although thousands of people travelled in them, there are few accounts of what the experience was like. Of one thing we can be certain from later accounts. These early steamships were exceedingly dirty, not with the bugs and excrement dirt of the long-range passenger sailing vessels, but from smuts and smoke and bits of coal. To travel on the open deck must have been a filthy experience and even the companion ways down to the best accommodation must have been as black as the outside of the carriages of steam railways used to be.

The use of steam vessels for packet and passenger services very rapidly expanded. By 1822 the *James Watt* was running a service between London and Leith. Soon every obvious route had its paddle packets, tugs were beginning to develop and a cross channel service was inaugurated. According to Geoffrey Body's book, *British Paddle Steamers*, in 1825 50,000 people travelled by the new services from London to Margate and soon over a million people a year were to travel by steamer on the Thames on one service or another. By 1827, according to Robin Craig, the historian of nineteenth century merchant shipping, there were 225 steamships registered as of British ports under the Merchant Shipping Act, yet there were only 624 ten years later. The short service routes were soon saturated, and it was to be a very long time before steamships could be operated economically, albeit with a mail subsidy, on even the most lucrative of ocean passenger routes, the North Atlantic, and not until the 1860s was the steamer finally to offer fatal competition to sailing vessels in general long-range trade.

But experiments with steamships on long routes started very early. The classic instance is the voyage of the American auxiliary sailing ship *Savannah*, which crossed to Liverpool in 1819. She was followed in 1821–22 by a British auxiliary, the *Rising Star*, which crossed the Atlantic well to the south, but in a westerly direction while on a delivery voyage to Chile. Then in 1824, the *Enterprise* took seventeen passengers to Calcutta. 'The cabins, of which there are 20, are fitted with every convenience' a contemporary Canadian newspaper put it – but nevertheless it must have been an arduous journey. Seven years later, in 1831 the *Sarah Jane* made a steam-assisted passage to Australia and in June, July and August 1833 the most difficult of all crossings, the east to west passage of the North Atlantic, was first achieved by a steam-assisted vessel, the *Cape Breton*, built at Blackwall earlier in the same year, which made a passage from Plymouth to Sydney, Nova Scotia. Other steam-assisted crossings followed.

But it was not until 1838 that a trans-Atlantic service under steam was seriously started with the crossing of two vessels. The first, the *Sirius*, was the first vessel to cross the Atlantic under continuous steam power. She carried forty passengers, eleven in 'the cabins' at thirty-five guineas each, eight in second class cabins at twenty guineas each and twenty-one in steerage accommodation at eight guineas. The second vessel was the *Great Western*, one of the many products of the genius of the builder of the Great Western Railway, Isambard Kingdom Brunel, and the first of the three great steamships with which he was to be associated. She was to make sixty-four crossings of the North Atlantic and on the strength of this achievement she has been called the first Atlantic liner.

CHAPTER FIVE

The Paddle Liners

The *Great Western* marked the beginning of a new era of steam. Cramped, rough, uncomfortable and inconvenient as the accommodation in her and her successors for the next twenty years may seem to have been in the light of the luxury that was to follow in the last thirty years of the century, it was at once very much better than the ordinary accommodation offered at sea in sailing vessels. The passenger now was an important commercial asset, to be cultivated and treated as such. The very beginning of the era of mass travel had arrived. Passengers making trans-oceanic voyages were no longer either drawn from a few relatively rich people who were provided with space to furnish as they liked and with a place at table, or helpless fugitives from the economic or social storm forced to travel willy nilly at the lowest possible cost, ignorant and often accustomed to a near animal existence. Passengers now increasingly were ordinary people travelling for business or pleasure, or if they were emigrants seeking to better themselves in new lands they had, under the successive Passenger Acts, to be carried under conditions of reasonable decency. In a trade which almost at once became highly competitive, the object of competition for the first time in history was the patronage of a great number of passengers and the commodities to be marketed soon became comfort and service. The era of luxury at sea which was to end only with the jet aeroplane in the early 1960s was making its first uncertain appearance.

Moreover, because progress was soon rapid and because accommodation became a marketable commodity with big money at stake, many more detailed descriptions of ships' cabins and saloons began to appear. They were mostly inspired for advertising purposes and printed either as accounts of the latest wonder, or in the latter part of the century, designed to show how much more the vessels of the 80s and 90s had to offer than had those of the 40s and 50s. But these detailed descriptions of the discomforts of the first liners as compared with those of the third and fourth generation succeed in painting pictures of the *Great Western's* immediate successors which show them as a tremendous and sudden advance on almost all their predecessors in the accommodation they offered. To travel by sea ceased quickly to be an intensively uncomfortable, often boring major adventure of uncertain duration and became quite suddenly reasonably safe, reasonably predictable in duration and quite tolerably comfortable by the standards of the times.

The long, narrow central saloon with the 'staterooms' – the passengers' cabins – opening off it on either side which was inherited from the sailing ship and the packet steamer persisted until the 1870s, but it became steadily bigger and more luxurious. It still doubled as a dining room and main recreation space but in the *Great Western*, for example, it was 75 feet long and 21 feet wide, and it had a headroom of 9 feet against a maximum of 7 feet in most earlier vessels, both sail and steam. The main saloon was decorated with painted panels showing country scenes and subjects 'representative of the arts and sciences' and 'parties grouped, or engaged in elegant sports and amusements'. These were described as being 'in the style of Watteau' and were executed by a Royal Academician called Parris. This was the beginning of the interior decoration which was later to become perhaps the chief original feature of the furnishing of passenger ships.

The 128 staterooms of the *Great Western* were no longer confined to the underside of the poop and a deck below. They were built in several different parts of the vessel, in the 'tween decks and in deck houses on the upper deck. The main cabin on the upper deck was 59 feet long. The cabins were all of one class and the fare from Bristol to New York was 35 guineas, children half price. It was a very expensive way of travelling. To obtain a steward the passenger no longer had to open his stateroom door and yell, a system which placed women passengers at a grave disadvantage. Each cabin was fitted with a bell rope and by a system of cranks and wires one of two bells, together with a rocking indicator to show which cabin was calling, was set in motion in the stewards' quarters. A card describing the working of this bell system was displayed for each passenger to read. Altogether the seven passengers, including one woman, who crossed the Atlantic on the *Great Western's* historic maiden voyage must have been spoiled to death, especially as besides the stewards she carried a pioneering stewardess.

A contemporary and rival of the *Great Western* in the latter's early years in the Atlantic trade was the *Liverpool*, a vessel of just over 1000 tons, a little smaller than the *Great Western*. The *Liverpool Mercury* described her accommodation at length in 1838 in the following terms:

'The "main or after cabin" is a splendid apartment of 58 feet in length, and 28 feet 9 inches in width at one end, slightly narrowing to 22 feet 4 inches at the stern; it is 8 feet in height to the beams, and $8\frac{1}{2}$ feet between them . . . The state-rooms are exceedingly handsome and commodious. There are in this cabin, sixteen in number, each with two berths or beds, with the exception of two, which are fitted, for the peculiar accommodation of a party, with three beds. They are well lighted from the roofs and sides by patent lights, those on the sides, serving also, on being opened as ventilators. The colouring of these rooms is a warm delicate pink, with gorgeous damask silk hangings to correspond, of French white, with crimson satin stripes. At the broadest or midship end of this main cabin is the ladies' retiring or private room, where several beds are also elegantly fitted up, and every convenience for the comfort and adornment of "the fair" is provided . . . There are tanks in abundance, in addition to which water will be daily and hourly distilled by an apparatus fixed for the purpose, and will undergo filtration, so as to be equal in purity and coolness to that of the "crystal well" of the hermit. It may be added that in the main cabin, including the ladies' staterooms, and the sofas, no fewer than fifty beds are provided.

'The "fore cabin" is 45 feet in length, by from 29 feet 4 inches to 23 feet 10 inches in width, and has eight dormitories or state-rooms on each side. This room is fitted

42

in a style somewhat different to the other, but scarcely less beautiful or costly. The walls are empanelled in rosewood and other woods, with rich style, and separated by circular-topped pilasters.'

The reference to the sofas in the main cabin is an interesting one. Many early steamers increased their passenger sleeping accommodation by fitting shelves, one above the other on the inside of the slope of the counter. These were normally used as seats and were padded and cushioned accordingly but when necessary they could double up as berths, when curtains were fitted to give some small degree of privacy. Because of their position in the extreme stern of the vessel and (at a slightly later period) over the screw, they must have been intensely uncomfortable in bad weather. Indeed only the most hardened and experienced travellers can have used them without becoming exhausted in a day or two. It was, of course, not possible to retire to bed until the last passengers had left the saloon and it was necessary to rise before the stewards laid the breakfast. There were definite rules as to when lights should be put out which were a legacy of sailing ship days and evidence of the traumatic fear of fire which has, quite rightly, haunted the history of the passenger vessel down to the present day. One company at the beginning of the 1840s required that the cook's fire and ship's company lights be extinguished at 9 p.m., fires and lights in the saloon and all cabins by 11 p.m. The lower scuttles were fastened at 8 p.m., dinner was served at 4 p.m. and tea at 7 p.m. so that passengers did not have to suffer the smells of a recent meal when they went to bed on the sofas. Besides oil lamps, there were candles fitted in the usual weighted gimbal mountings so that they stood more or less upright but which must have guttered and dripped all the time. Often one candle was suspended in a hole in a cabin wall so that it served two cabins.

On one of her early eastward-bound passages, the *Liverpool* carried a passenger who was to play a major role in the development of the steam passenger liner. He was Samuel Cunard, a Nova Scotian from Halifax, who came to Britain to set up a company to build four steamships to run regularly in the North Atlantic passenger trade. By mid-1840 his first vessel, the paddle steamer *Britannia* of 1,156 tons gross had begun her service. She carried mail and she and her sisters received a subsidy which made their operation economically possible. She carried a crew of eighty-nine officers and men and the former were accommodated in houses on the deck. Here also was a shelter for the cows which provided the passengers with fresh milk. There was accommodation for 115 passengers, all first class, in cabins on the main deck. According to some accounts in the extreme stern in place of the sofas were bathrooms, and there were smoking rooms and sitting rooms in deckhouses. The staterooms were small with narrow, curtained bunks, one above the other, the whole six feet wide by perhaps twelve feet long. There were two basins and jugs with a little mirror above them and a shelf with a water-carafe and glasses, a hard sofa and pegs on which to hang clothes. There was no wardrobe and passengers were expected to live out of their trunks. The whole was lit with one porthole or a lamp at night.

Charles Dickens was an early passenger in the *Britannia* and he wrote disparagingly of her accommodation, not by comparison with what had gone before at sea but with standards of comfort on land. He reported that the smoking room was in fact only a compartment over the boiler, shared with stokers hoisting ashes. The few books on board were kept under lock and key, there was no musical instrument and no bathroom. The only walking space was on top of a deckhouse and to get to your meals you had to climb over the backs of the long bench seats at the saloon tables. Dickens might have added that to relieve yourself in the *Britannia* you had to use a lavatory in one of the little hutches built into the sponsons abaft the paddles – the arrangement can be seen very well in the *Reliant* at the National Maritime Museum which has fittings which in many ways resemble those of the vessels of half a century earlier.

The saloons of these early steamers, the main place of recreation for the passengers, were a very important feature of the vessel. They were heated by coal stoves, possibly by only one (as in the *Britannia* according to Dickens) but more likely by two or three. In bad weather the poop skylights above had to be closed and protected with wooden breakwaters and then the saloon would become very stuffy. The state rooms opened either directly on to the saloon or on to one of the series of little passages leading off the saloon and at right angles to it. There was usually one long table with a form on each side. Like a very old-fashioned tram-car's seats, this form had a back which could be swung across it from side to side so that the seat could look away from the table for the passengers' recreational purposes. It was placed sufficiently far from the table for passengers to walk along to the centre without much inconvenience even when wearing a woman's dress of the 1840s. Men, like Dickens, usually stepped over the back. The benches were usually covered with artificial leather which was shiny and slippery and it has been recorded that passengers who had not correctly anticipated a roll of the vessel vanished under the table. The food served was cooked in a galley on deck, as in sailing ships, and as with a sailing vessel the hot prepared food had to be carried in the open on the first part of its journey to the table. From the first, however, the food was as varied and well-prepared as the preserving achievements of the age and the facilities provided by coal stoves allowed.

Conditions for passengers in some of these mid-century steamers are well-described in the journal of a landsman who made a passage to the West Indies in one of them in 1847. He travelled in the *Forth*, which was no run down old-timer but a nearly new steamer of the Royal Mail Steam Packet Company which received a substantial subsidy to operate the mail service to the Caribbean. Her accommodation was very similar to that shown in the plan of her sister ship, the *Tweed*, which appears among the illustrations at the end of this chapter, (Plate 48). She was one of fourteen vessels built to start the company's operations in 1841. By the terms of the mail contract she had to have engines of 450 horsepower and be capable of mounting guns and she was built to a general specification laid down by the Admiralty. Nevertheless, great though the improvement was over sailing ship conditions, the journal records some gloomy times on board her:

'23rd January. I went to my berth early last night, in order to have a good night's rest as I had slept but little the two previous nights; but about eleven o'clock, in consequence of the ship working so much, the deck above my berth began to leak, and soaked the bedclothes, so that I had to turn out and dress. I had a bed made up on a sofa in the saloon, but after I got to sleep and had slept a few hours, I was aroused by the water coming in upon me, so I had to get up and walk the deck, which I did at about five o'clock. I remained on deck about a quarter of an hour, and then one of the officers offered me his berth into which I got and slept soundly until about eight o'clock . . . On going on deck after dinner today, we found, much to our chagrin, that the engines had again broken down, and that we were again lying to with a S.W. gale, which in our present position is not very satisfactory, especially as there is every appearance of the gale increasing; there are no amusements on tonight, as everyone is out of spirits in consequence of the delay. We have not been able to learn the extent of the damage, as the engineers are very close on this point; one of them told us that the stoppage was caused by the end of some person's cigar having got between the piston and the cylinder, and so stopped the engine; but I ought to observe that this person dislikes smoking.'

Quoted in 'Travellers by Sea', National Maritime Museum, 1962

The next really big further improvement in accommodation took place when the first American company began to compete in the North Atlantic trade. This was the Collins Line, and, like the Royal Mail, it operated with subsidised vessels capable of some measure of conversion for war purposes. For almost the first time cabins were carpeted and passengers no longer had to dress for dinner with the aid of a single mirror. For the first time also they did not shiver as they did so. The first Collins liner was the *Atlantic*, built in New York in 1849. Considerably larger than the *Britannia* her accommodation carried on to the North Atlantic the tradition of comfort and luxury established from the first by American steamboats. When she arrived in Liverpool on May 10th 1850 at the end of her maiden passage across the North Atlantic the *Illustrated London News* described her accommodation in the following terms:

'Her saloon is 67 feet long by 20 feet wide. Her interior fittings are truly elegant, the woodwork being of white holly, satinwood, rosewood, &c., so combined and diversified as to present an exceedingly rich and costly appearance. In the drawing room the ornaments consist of costly mirrors, bronze-work, stained glass, paintings, &c. Between the panels connecting the staterooms are the arms of the different states of the confederacy painted in the highest style of art, and framed with bronze-work. The pillars between are inlaid with mirrors, framed with rosewood, and at the top and bottom are bronzed sea-shells of costly workmanship. In the centre of each are allegorical figures representing the ocean mythology of the ancients, in bronze and burnished gold. The ceiling is elaborately wrought, carved and gilded. The cabin windows in the stern are of painted glass, having representations of New York, Boston and Philadelphia painted on each. There is in addition another apartment equally beautifully arranged and ornamented, for the exclusive use of ladies. Both apartments are heated by steam, an improvement now for the first time introduced in steamships. The dining room (60 feet long) is furnished in an equally elegant style with the drawing room. The staterooms, which are light and airy, are beautifully furnished and ornamented, and combine every convenience that practical science and experience could suggest. It would occupy more space than can be spared to detail the magnificence of the furniture of the

Atlantic; the carpets are of the richest description; the table-slabs are of Brocatelli marble. Each stateroom has an elegant sofa; the berths are of satinwood, and the curtains of rich damask.'

Though due allowance must be made for journalistic exaggeration and for the fact that the writers of these glowing descriptions were accustomed by our standards to very poor living conditions, nevertheless in the 1850s a new era in accommodation at sea had begun and at last the stern cabins of the *Charlotte Jane*, improved upon by the accommodation of the *Great Western* and the *Britannia*, were to cease to represent the ultimate in comfort and convenience available.

The potential earnings in the relatively short range North Atlantic passenger trade, backed up with mail subsidies, made possible the profitable operation of paddle steamships driven by side-lever engines, even though the engines were very inefficient in terms of cost per mile steamed and the prodigious consumption of coal by the boilers left little in reserve at the end of each passage. But such vessels and the early screw steamships could not operate in long range trade, not only because it was not profitable to do so, but also because the distance between coaling stations and the total absence of coaling stations on the long runs between Cape Town and Australia, Australia and the west coast of the North American continent, meant that it was not physically possible to steam over these great distances.

But, as we have already said, the discovery of gold in Australia in the early 1850s led to a great increase in passenger trade and a demand for faster passages. The fast sailing ships benefited accordingly – more and more high class sailing vessels were placed on the route. Obviously vessels assisted by steam might be able to command fares high enough to make their operation profitable if they could, by steaming through those areas of the oceans where the climatic conditions made the sailing vessel predictably liable to delay and by sailing where the powerful and predictable trade winds and the westerlies of the southern ocean made sailing fast and easy, make passages regularly shorter than those of purely sailing vessels. Such steamships would take in coal at the Cape Verde Islands and at Cape Town and early logs show that the art of commercially successful operation lay in relating the power developed by the engine, and therefore the coal consumed, to the conditions of wind and sea and the amount of sail set.

Something like luxury first came to the Australian trade when a vessel built in anticipation of purchase by the American Collins Line was diverted to Australia. She was the *Golden Age*, a wooden paddle steamer of almost 3,000 tons, built by William H. Brown of New York. She was purchased by the New York and Australian Navigation Company and made a passage from New York to Sydney via Liverpool in 1852–3. She had accommodation for 1,200 passengers, including 600 in the steerage. The first class passengers travelled in one of three saloons, two of them were finished with panelling in rose, satin and zebra woods interspersed with mirrors. The curtains and soft furnishings were of crimson and gold plush. In the upper saloon the walls were finished in white and gold. It was said that in this saloon there were two 'family rooms', one finished in gold and the other in blue. Another luxurious early vessel in the trade was the *Royal Charter*, in due course to be wrecked disastrously off Anglesey when inward bound from Australia with the loss of almost everybody on board. She is described as having two large bathrooms for the use of the saloon passengers and one very large bathroom for the communal use of those in the steerage.

Despite unsuccessful experiments and financial losses, the steamer, first in the form of an auxiliary and then as a fully-powered vessel, had come to offer competition to the ordinary long range sailing vessel, though not to eliminate her for nearly eighty years. In 1843 Brunel launched the *Great Britain,* a screw-driven vessel. She demonstrated clearly the efficiency and practicality of this method of propulsion over and above the paddle steamer but it was to be another twenty years before the last first-class paddle steamer was to be built for the Atlantic passenger service. In the meanwhile, the *Great Eastern,* the monster of the late 1850s, also a creation of Brunel, was built as a vessel propelled partly by paddles. The last major paddle liner was the Cunarder *Scotia* of 1862, and she was something of a delayed anachronism—she was originally intended to be launched in 1856. More typical in time and very typical of the last great paddle ships was the *Persia,* built for the Cunard Line under the stimulus of Collins Line competition in 1855. Of 3,300 tons she was the first iron paddle steamer on the Atlantic route. Her immense side-lever engines developed over 3,600 indicated horse-power. She carried 200 first class passengers and 50 second class and she made a succession of record voyages that not only finally established the Cunard Line's supremacy over the Collins Line, but also inaugurated a new standard of express passenger service.

The passengers in the *Persia* travelled in considerable comfort. A detailed drawing of her accommodation is in the draught room at the National Maritime Museum and parts of it are reproduced at the end of this chapter (Plates 51 and 52). They show in great detail the accommodation of the last of the first generation of crack steam passenger ships, the ultimate in accommodation at sea in the 1850s and early 1860s.

CHAPTER SIX

The Travelling Palaces

The paddle steamer, even at its finest in the *Persia* and the *Scotia* of 1862, had serious limitations. The machinery was inefficient, that is, a great deal of coal was burned for every mile steamed and the method of propulsion, the paddle wheel, was also very inefficient. In the great side-lever engines massive weights moved up and down, stopping and reversing on every stroke, setting up stresses in the structure of the machinery. The parts had to be very strong and therefore very heavy to resist these stresses and great amounts of power were absorbed in the process. The paddles were even less efficient when used in bad weather, when they might alternately be out of the water for much of the time, and they were very liable to be damaged. The paddler's real role was as a vessel for working in shallow water, as on the rivers of the United States and on the great rivers of the Indian sub-continent and in Burma. She was also very useful when extreme manoeuvrability was required, as in certain kinds of towing work. As long as steam power was applied only to wooden paddle steamers its effectiveness in even middle-range trade was really confined to subsidised operations on high density passenger routes.

The first stage of development was the general adoption of the screw propeller, which gave more drive per horsepower applied to the shaft, but the stresses set up in a screw-driven hull were such as to make this form of propulsion not really suitable for wooden vessels, which leaked and aged rapidly when it was fitted. There were exceptions to this. Very strongly-built wooden whalers with low-powered steam engines were to be very successful later in the century. Small iron ships were in use in the 1830s, but the material was not readily available in the sizes necessary for constructing bigger ships and it was not until the *Great Britain*, built between 1839 and 1843, that a really large iron ship – at the time by far the largest in the world – was launched. She truly represents the beginnings of the real transition from paddles to screw propeller for she was laid down to be a paddler and finished as the world's first large ocean-going iron screw steamship. After early and rather uncertain beginnings on the North Atlantic route, in 1852 after an extensive refit she began the first of thirty-two successful round voyages to Australia. She could then accommodate 730 passengers and she actually had 650 passengers on board on her first passage to Australia. In her Australian trade role she was the first large steamship to have a saloon extending from side to side of the vessel, and she set a standard of accommodation which was not to be regularly surpassed for twenty years. But she was operated as an auxiliary, that is, she sailed without using her engines for long distances in areas of steady, predictable, favourable winds. Her success did not therefore mean that the steamship had become an economic proposition in ordinary long range ocean trade. The *Great Britain*, of course, has now returned to Bristol after more than eighty years in the sub-Antarctic as a hulk. She is now undergoing partial restoration to the form in which she was first fitted out.

A passenger, Miss Rachel Henning, who made a passage to Australia in the *Great Britain* left an account of life on board which does credit to the vessel. She wrote:

'The cabin is so light that I can read well in bed, and the lamp shines into my berth, so, that being the case, I have nailed up a moreen bag just within reach of my hand, and put a little store of books into it; also my lantern, matches, camphor, etc . . . The bag of tools is worth its weight in gold. I have driven innumerable nails for Mrs. Bronchordt and myself, and though the steward did come and inquire if the carpenter was in our cabin yesterday, as he was particularly wanted, no one has found fault with the nails, and the cupboard which Mr Boyce screwed up behind the funnel has never been seen and is most useful. . . . The "ladies' boudoir" which they talk about is a nice little room enough, but rather dark and chiefly used by the children. I shall probably sit in the saloon, most likely where I am sitting now by the table just opposite the entrance to my cabin.' (See Plate 53)

Then, writing of a storm:

' . . . (The *Great Britain*) behaved admirably, took in very little water, and came up as stiff as possible after every roll. Several seas came on board, however; one broke into the saloon and thence into the cabins, one of which was three feet deep in water, the steward mopped and dipped it out in buckets. . . . You cannot think how dirty everything gets; hands, clothes, everything is black . . . I was very sorry to say goodbye to the *Great Britain* and her captain when we sailed from Melbourne. She is a splendid ship, and I am sure we all have reason to speak well of her.'

Quoted in 'Women under Sail' by Basil Greenhill and Ann Giffard, Newton Abbot, 1970

The custom of nailing up bags in cabins seems to have been fairly common. Several contemporary diaries refer to the practice, which seems to have been accepted as a way of providing storage where drawers were inadequate and often inaccessible. A handbill advertising the *Great Britain* sailing for Australia gives some very interesting sidelights on the conditions of travel for passengers:

'DIETARY. SALOON, First Class, will be found with a first-rate Table. SECOND CLASS Passengers will have to supply themselves with Bed, Bedding, Linen, Soap, but are found with Crockery, Glass, &c, by the Ship, divided into messes, and provided with stewards; the passengers are, however, expected to promote their own and each other's comfort by giving every assistance in their power . . .
Passengers are expected to pay for any Crockery or Glass they may break from want of proper care.

THIRD CLASS AND STEERAGE. – In these Cabins passengers must provide their own Utensils and Bedding. The Articles required are Beds, Bedding, Towels, Knife and Fork each, Tea and Table spoons, a Tin or Wooden Plate, a Drinking Can, a Coffee or Tea Cup, Tin Quart Pot and Keg to hold 3 Gallons of Water. Small stores such as Ham, Bacon, Pickles, Sauces, can be purchased from the Purser at moderate prices. Price Lists are placed in various parts of the Vessel . . .

BERTHS

The Saloon state rooms contain two and three berths, except the family rooms. In the Second, two and three and four berths; but rooms to suit applicants will be made if specially arranged for. Persons engaging accommodation for themselves or others, will be held responsible for one-half the passage money, and be required to pay the same, whether they have made a deposit or not. Gunpowder, Lucifer Matches, and Combustibles of every description, strictly prohibited . . .'

One of the earliest steam vessels in the Australian passenger trade was the *Calcutta* operated by the General Screw Steam Shipping Company. Like the *Great Britain* she operated in this long range trade as an auxiliary sailing without her engine for substantial parts of the long Australian voyage. The *Calcutta* was also constructed of iron, by C. J. Mare and Company at West Ham in 1852. Her first voyage was an experimental one to India during which she steamed for much of her time at sea. On this voyage she carried a crew of 110, including 20 stewards and servants. The ratio of stewards and servants to passengers was about one to four and the service available to the passengers must have seemed to them quite remarkable. Her second voyage was to Australia. An extract from an advertisement put out by her owners reveals a good deal about conditions of the trade in which pioneer steamers, some of which had suffered disasters, were competing with established and well known sailing vessels which, as has been indicated in Chapter Two, began after 1850 to offer relatively good conditions for passengers:

'The attention of the Public is requested to the splendid passages of these Steamers, on the Line between Southampton and Calcutta. The *Queen of the South*, which left with the Mails for Australia April 4th, was the pioneer ship of the Indian Mail Steam Ship Line, *via* the Cape of Good Hope; and returned from Calcutta to Plymouth on the 26th February last, (her third voyage) punctually *to an hour*. A significant fact, and worthy of note, when it is considered that the distance is about 27,000 miles by sea, and that she had to stop at seven ports outward, and eight homeward. This feat has not been accomplished by any other ships in the world but by those belonging to the General Screw Steam Shipping Company. She is a sister ship to the *Argo*, which made the voyage to Melbourne in 64 days, and home by Cape Horn in the same period; thus literally circumnavigating the globe in 128 days. This has yet to be equalled.

'It is deemed but just to the public to state these facts, that they may know what this Company's magnificent vessels have done, and thus come to a rational conclusion as to what they are likely to do on the Australian Service; and it is also essential in order that this Company's vessels may not be confounded with others that have not been so fortunate.

'The *Calcutta* is sister ship to the *Argo, Queen of the South* and *Lady Jocelyn*.

'Her accommodations are of a most superior description, including superb Saloons fully furnished. Bath Rooms, and many other comforts for Passengers are on board. The Cabins are provided with everything necessary for the voyage. Beds and Bedding, Linen, Soap, Lights, and Towels, included. Stewards and

Stewardesses are engaged, who will be in constant attendance. Wine, Spirits, and beer may be obtained on board at moderate prices.'

The *Calcutta* had a screw propellor which could be lifted from the water when she was sailing. One passenger commented:

'Yesterday the wind freshened so that they took up the screw and the ship went on under canvas. I thought it a much pleasanter motion but we rolled about a good deal more, and there were several alarming smashes of crockery, and some of the passengers having, contrary to orders, opened their portholes, the lower deck was streaming with water, so the First Officer had all the handles taken off the portholes, and now they cannot be opened at all.'

A few years after the *Great Britain* and while this vessel was still employed in the North Atlantic trade, the *City of Glasgow* was launched. She was an iron screw steamer built by Tod and MacGregor of Glasgow and she became the pioneer vessel of the once famous Inman Line. More than one historian of the shipping industry has gone on record as saying that she was the first really successful ocean steamship – that is, a vessel able to pay her way without Government Mail subsidy. But of course she did this only on the North Atlantic route in successful competition with the sailing packets for their class of trade. She had a spar deck covering part of the main deck and forming, according to a contemporary Glasgow newspaper:

'a magnificent promenade in fine weather, and in foul weather the main deck accorded ample space for recreation, perfectly lighted and ventilated and protected from rain or spray. On each side are ranged the staterooms, leaving 16 feet clear in the centre. The height between the decks is 7 feet.

'The accommodation for each class of passengers is admirable and most complete. She will carry fifty-two cabin, or first class, passengers, eighty-five second class, and 400 steerage emigrants. . . . Two of the state rooms for first class passengers have four berths in each, all the others have only two. The state rooms for second class passengers have four or eight berths in each. The state rooms for ladies are so capacious that they may be used as sitting rooms, should they chose to retire from the main cabins. The latter is an apartment of noble dimensions, and will be elegantly fitted up, and furnished with a well assorted library. The walls will be decorated with panellings representing views of places of interest on both sides of the Atlantic.'

The *City of Glasgow* was a pioneer vessel in another and very important respect. She was the first regular trans-Atlantic steamer to carry emigrants. Though the bulk of the emigrant trade continued to be carried for another ten years in the empty 'tween decks of westward bound timber ships to Canadian ports for distribution by river steamer and railroad throughout the Northern states, the *City of Glasgow's* entry into this business on her runs to Philadelphia marked the beginning of the end of this form of passenger travel at sea. It is recorded that William Inman, the driving force behind the new line, together with his wife made a passage in one of the first Inman steamers fitted out to carry emigrants for the purpose of 'ameliorating the discomforts and evil hitherto but too common in emigrant ships.' This passage served a philanthropic purpose. Certainly from the inauguration of this service the opportunities for emigrants to travel in relative comfort steadily improved.

The *City of Glasgow* soon had her imitators. The Montreal Ocean Steamship Company, familiarly known as the Allan Line, began its operations with the *Canadian,* also an iron screw steamship in 1854. In 1854 also the Company obtained a mail contract and from that time forward its services were developed as a screw steamship company and it too was to play a large part in the demise of the wooden sailing ship in the emigrant trade. The Allan Line was also notable for the fact that one of its steamers, the *Hibernian* of 1861, followed the example of the *City of Glasgow* in having a spar deck, that is the covering over the main deck, in her case over the whole deck from stem to stern, which enabled the passengers to use that deck in heavy weather. Other companies soon joined in the North Atlantic passenger trade, including the National Line which, like Inman's and the Allan Line, competed less with the big Cunard paddlers than with the sailing packets in the Atlantic trade. This line's vessels carried large numbers of emigrants and large cargoes, and one of them, the *Italy* of 1868, was an historic vessel, the first compound engine steamship to be put on the North Atlantic route.

Three products of nineteenth century technology had to be used together before the steamship could be used on all world routes in competition with the sailing ship. The large scale production of iron in large dimensions made possible the iron vessel. The iron vessel made possible the use of the screw propeller, not merely more efficient than the paddle in the simple sense that it worked whatever the weather and however much the vessel rolled (though it has always been thrown out of the water in a light vessel when she pitches) and was not susceptible to damage in the same way, but more efficient in the technical sense in that it delivered more thrust per unit of power applied to the shaft than a paddle ever could. The driving of a screw propellor shaft was an ideal function for the economical compound engine, able to deliver much more power per unit of coal consumed and occupy much less space than its simple predecessors.

The compound engine was the key to the success of the steamship after 1860 and its development and manufacture in Britain was one of the keys to British commercial and political ascendancy in its turn in the next forty years. In a compound engine the steam once it had expanded in the cylinder was not condensed and recovered as water but admitted to a second and in due course to a third cylinder where it expanded again, providing drive for a second and a third piston operating the same crankshaft. Such an engine, once the practical problems had been overcome, could operate on half the fuel consumption of a simple engine for the same distance steamed and power developed. It was no longer impossible to carry the coal necessary for the long ocean hauls away from coaling stations, no longer necessary to buy so much coal at high bunkering station prices or to give up space to coal bunkers on board the vessel to a degree which made it impossible to carry sufficient cargo to make the vessel pay her way. The hey-day of the steamship and the great days of the passenger liner all over the world came with the compound engine, so completely and dramatically that the expansion in steamship building and the consequent demand for coal at the beginning of the 1870s drove the price of the fuel for a few years up to levels – in some cases three times as high as in the mid-1860s – which put some budding steamship companies out of business before they had really begun. Though the prime movers changed from the recipro-cating steam engine, the hey-day lasted about eighty years, from 1870 to 1950. In the rest of this chapter we are concerned with accommodation in vessels during the first thirty of these. This was an era when the United States played little or no part in the development of passenger transport at sea. After the era of the wooden paddler, American shipowners dropped out of the passenger routes and American capital and business enterprise busied itself with other forms of commerce.

In this period two further great technical developments were to take place, the application of steel in shipbuilding, which gave greater strength for lighter weight, and the adoption of twin screws and with them the final end of the 'steam and sail' era and the abandonment of the use of the masts and yards which gave to the steam vessel of the nineteenth century an air of elegance and grace which was never to be recovered in quite the same way. With these developments and the rising prosperity of the British and North American peoples, the first era of mass travel had at last arrived and with it totally new conceptions of commercially competitive comfort for passengers at sea. Moreover, by the 1870s photography had become a fairly simple and reliable affair and a generally accepted medium for conveying information. So from the 1870s onwards, more and more photographs are available in the National Maritime Museum's historic photographic archive and in other collections showing passenger accommodation (but not crews' accommodation), and by the 1890s, they become a feast, almost a surfeit of Victoriana. The story of how accommodation, under the stimulus of commercial necessity, was pushed towards a luxury which in some cases ran riot is best conveyed by these photographs, of which a selection appears at the end of this chapter. But first there are a number of developments not apparent in the photographs of which some account should be given.

The adoption of screw propulsion meant that the engines could be lower in the vessel and the compact compound engine, which occupied much less of the space amidships formerly taken up by the paddler's engines, left room above and around it for passenger accommodation. By the 1870s, the upper decks of steamships had begun to resemble a train running through a cutting, the long, narrow deckhouses which stretched from end to end of the vessel and contained much of the accommodation outside the stern cabin corresponded to the coaches, while the high solid bulwarks, as high as the deckhouses themselves, resembled the sides of a low cutting. But in the early 1870s for the first time, ship's accommodation began to break away from the dominance of the long-dying sailing ship tradition of the great stern cabin. The best accommodation began to be fitted amidships. There thus developed a new shape for a passenger ship, high in the middle and low at the ends, the reverse of the classic sheer of the working boat and the sailing vessel. Her passengers and crew became less aware of the sea and less linked with it. No longer could a sea sweep a vessel's main deck. As superstructures grew higher, so the sea was further and further away from the passenger and less important to him. Soon the pattern developed of assisting and encouraging him to forget it altogether.

The pioneer of the new type of vessel was the *Oceanic,* built in 1870, needless to say for the pacesetting North Atlantic service. She made possible the concept of the steamship as a travelling palace, which was to be slowly adopted on other routes and to persist until the last years of large scale passenger transport by sea. It was a pattern established by the White Star Line, the *Oceanic* and by the shipbuilding firm of Harland and Wolff at Belfast.

In the *Oceanic*, the narrow deckhouses and high bulwarks were replaced by a completely new deck, covered over so that the covering deck itself provided yet another deck level, surrounded by railings so that any sea which came on board was not retained. She had a dining saloon which extended the full width of the ship, lit by skylights and much bigger side windows than any of her predecessors. The first class staterooms were extended aft on either side of the engine room trunk and forward at the sides of the cargo trunks. These staterooms were much bigger than any built into a regular passenger steamship before and almost every one had natural light from a porthole and the portholes themselves were larger than had been customary. The old business of yelling for the steward or yanking at the bell rope was ended for ever by the provision of electric bells in the cabins. In the dining saloon the old long table with benches with reversible backs was at last done away with and two large tables with a separate chair for each passenger replaced it. The second class passengers were accommodated on the same deck as the first class but abaft of them, in fact just where the first class passengers used traditionally to be accommodated. The third class were placed in the ends of the vessel. More lavatories were provided and they were nearer the sleeping accommodation. No longer was it necessary to choose between a chamber pot which might slop over with the vessel's motion and a journey across open decks in the middle of the night. The *Oceanic* had a straight stem, unlike the great majority of her predecessors, and this, together with her railed midships structure about the funnel, and her line of lifeboats gave her a modern appearance despite her low four-masted bark rig.

The revolutionary changes introduced in the *Oceanic* were quickly taken up by other companies. Further improvements followed. The cabins in the *Oceanic* were still lit by candles. Three years later the White Star Line introduced improved mineral oil lamps and in the *Adriatic* of 1872 a complete gas-lighting system fed from a gas plant alongside the engine room lit thirty jets in the first class saloon and the whole of the emigrants' accommodation. Only six years later the Inman liner, *City of Berlin,* was equipped with experimental electric light, six bulbs in the saloon and engine room, but it was not until the 1880s that electric light became at all common. The *Dynamic* of 1883, built by Harland and Wolff for the Belfast Steamship Company was one of the first vessels to be lighted throughout by electricity. Passenger vessels were well ahead of shore practice in the matter of electric lighting. Not until 1887 was the first theatre, the Savoy, lit by electricity. The first electric street lights did not appear until 1891. The *City of New York* and the *City of Paris* of the Inman Line in the late 1880s inaugurated twin-screws in first class North Atlantic passenger vessels and with them a new system of water-tight compartments and bulkheads which greatly increased the safety of the vessel. They, like most vessels of their period, had the forced draught ventilation which had been introduced by the White Star Line in the *Germanic* of 1874 and which enabled passengers to have some control over the temperature of their cabins and, in the case of emigrants, some fresh air. A contemporary, Henry Fry, who was a considerable figure in the history of Canada's merchant shipping, wrote of them in his *History of North Atlantic Steam Navigation,* published in 1896:

'The staterooms are large, lofty, and well-ventilated by fans and patent ventilators, which always admit fresh air, but exclude the sea, There are single and double beds which can be closed by day, as in a Pullman car, converting your room into a cosy little sitting-room . . . Neat wardrobes enable you to banish your portmanteau or trunks to the baggage-room . . . Each suite comprises a bedroom, with a brass bedstead, wardrobe etc, a sitting room, with sofa, easy chair, and table, a private lavatory and, in most cases, a private bath . . .

'To diminish seasickness you dine in a saloon near the middle of the ship, beautifully decorated with naiads, dolphins, tritons, and mermaids, lofty and bright. The arched roof is of glass 53 feet by 25 feet, and its height from the floor of the saloon to its crown is 20 feet. Besides the long dining table in the centre there are a number of small ones placed in alcoves on both sides for the use of families or parties of friends; revolving armchairs replace the benches, and electric lights the candlesticks with their lashings. If you enjoy a cigar or a pipe, a luxurious smoking room, 45 feet long, is provided, its walls and ceilings are panelled in black walnut, and its couches and chairs are covered with scarlet leather. There is an elegant "drawing-room" beautifully decorated and luxuriously furnished. The "library" with its 900 volumes is lined with oak wainscoting, with the names of distinguished authors carved on it in scrolls, and its stained glass windows inscribed with quotations referring to the sea. The kitchen is isolated in a steel shell, the odours from which are carried off by ventilating shafts into the funnels . . . Provision is made for divine service on the Sabbath day; at each end of the Saloon there is an oriel window built under the glass dome over the dining-saloon. The casement of one of these serves for a pulpit. The opposite one contains an organ.'

By the early 1890s the description of luxury on the North Atlantic route come thick and fast. Henry Fry wrote of the Cunarders *Campania* and *Lucania* of 1891:

'The dining saloon is a vast, lofty apartment, near the middle of the ship, 100 feet long, 62 feet broad and 10 feet high, capable of seating at dinner 430 passengers in revolving armchairs. The decorations are highly artistic: the ceiling is panelled in white and gold; the sides in Spanish mahogany; and the upholstering is in a dark rich red figured frieze velvet, with curtains to match. There are nooks and corners where small parties may dine in complete seclusion . . . For lighting as well as for ventilation there is a central well, 24 feet by 16 feet, carried up from the Saloon to above the awning deck, where it is covered by a curved dome of stained glass. The drawing room is a splendid apartment, 60 feet by 30 feet. The walls are in satinwood, relieved with cedar mouldings; the ceiling is in pine, decorated in light tones, in which old ivory and gilding prevail. The settees, ottomans, and chairs are upholstered in rich velvets and brocades, which, with a Persian carpet, brass firegrate, and hearth of Persian tiles, form a superb tout ensemble. A grand piano and an American organ are also provided.

'The library is 29 feet by 24 feet. The roof is very ornate, with electric lamps in each of the alternate panels. The columns supporting it are covered with Mecca and blue velvet. The walls are finished in rich carved mahogany, with Amboyna panels. Writing tables and chairs are arranged around them, and a handsome bookcase is filled with a choice library of books.

'The smoking-room is 40 feet by 32 feet. Its decorations are in the old Scottish baronial style, with chairs and tables to match.

'The state-rooms are lofty and well-ventilated. The old wooden coffin-like berth has been superseded by Hopkins' ''triptic'' beds, which are so constructed that the upper bed folds up against the bulkhead. The leeboard is movable, and being one-half the length of the bed can be fixed at either end or in the middle. There are rooms to suit all tastes; single and double berth cabins and family rooms. For those who do not mind the cost, there are suites of rooms fitted in satinwood and mahogany, with everything to match, parlour and bedrooms, the former fitted with tables and chairs after the style of a lady's boudoir; the latter fitted with a brass bedstead, hanging, wardrobe, etc. There are also staterooms fitted with a collapsible bedstead, or with one capable of being extended so as to form a double bed, and which, when used as a single one, may be converted into a couch and settee.

'The rooms for second class passengers are all placed abaft the machinery . . . The drawing-room is provided with a cottage piano . . .

'The steerage is fitted with iron portable berths.'

Of the *Teutonic* and the *Majestic* he wrote:

'The decorations in this splendid banqueting hall are in Renaissance style. Bas-relief figures of tritons and nymphs in gold and ivory colour gambol around, and the ceiling is decorated in a corresponding style. It is brilliantly lighted by electricity At either end there is beautifully carved oak cabinet work. The revolving arm-chairs and couches are sumptously upholstered. The Library is on the promenade deck. It is fitted with book-cases containing a good supply of standard books; writing tables are arranged around it, divided by racks for stationery, and at each end there are luxurious couches.

'The smoking-room is a cosy and handsome apartment. The woodwork is of rich dark mahogany; the walls are covered with embossed leather of the same tone, richly gilt. The panels are oil paintings, representing the ships of the Middle Ages, and there are handsome couches upholstered in leather. The main entrance to the Saloon, and the stairs leading to it, are of carved oak with white and gold ceilings . . .'

Eight years later the *Liverpool Daily Post* wrote almost ecstatically about the White Star Line's second *Oceanic*, 17,300 tons, the first ship to exceed the *Great Eastern* in size and a fitting closing to the century:

'. . . But much has been written already of the ship as a triumph of science; the more immediate purpose here is to speak of her as a triumph of art, as the last thing, so far, in the way of floating hotels . . . State rooms in scores to the right and to the left; now mahogany, now oak, now satinwood; now a mixture of any two or three of them, until the lavishness of everything became surfeiting, notwithstanding that the Louis Quinze style succeeded the Queen Anne, and the Queen Anne gave place to something "too utter" in decadent sumptousness. Three decks of these apartments, with lavatories of costly marble, suites of baths, and every other appurtenance of physical comfort placed conveniently here and there. It is the literal truth to say that the *Oceanic* is a Hotel Cecil afloat.

'The saloon is 80 feet by 64 feet. The central glass dome is 21 feet square and is divided up by golden ribs and filled in with ground glass of a pearly appearance.'

But perhaps there was one more word to say about steamships' accommodation in the nineteenth century. It was said in a description of the *Saxon*, launched by Harland and Wolff in 1900 for the Union Castle Line and employed not on the North Atlantic route but in service to South Africa:

'The first class library is situated on the Bridge Deck, and is reached by way of a superb entrance hall of Polish oak. This entrance hall and the passages are copies from the choir stall of the Gothic Cathedral of Ulm in Germany . . . In the bookcase there is a selection of books carefully chosen to suit all lines of thought.'

So much for the crack passenger route of the world which set the pace and the standards. The introduction of the compound engined iron or steel screw steamship with the bulk of her accommodation amidships took longer on the rest of the world's long distance sea routes, but after the first *Oceanic*, it was only a matter of time before this class of vessel was very widely adopted. The greater comforts for passengers were an especial boon on the long voyages to Australia, New Zealand and the Far East and it was on these routes that the introduction of refrigeration in the food stores in the 1870s made a very marked difference in the standards of passenger travel. Not only did the travelling farmyard with its attendant smells and other disadvantages, vanish but the whole standard of feeding, particularly for emigrant passengers was raised to much healthier levels.

Not until the late 70s and the beginning of the 80s were competitive through sailings from London to Sydney introduced and, as has already been said, these services ran in rivalry with steel passenger-carrying sailing ships, using the Cape of Good Hope route and offering passages at markedly lower fares.

In the United States the rapid expansion of the railroads reduced the relative importance of the steamer, even in an era of economic and population expansion. But, despite the abandonment of the classic deep sea passenger routes by American enterprise (in 1870 Britain had 1,202,134 tons of steam shipping registered, the United States only 192,544 tons in foreign trade), the steamship continued to play an important part in the development of the continent, and the companies which operated the river and short sea passenger routes remained faithful to the paddle steamer. There were very good reasons for this. The North American short service passenger steamer was the heir to a tradition of luxury which could not be abandoned without financial disaster. She operated in relatively sheltered waters and she loaded and discharged often in very shallow berths. As a contemporary put it in the early years of this century, the problem became to 'construct a six-storey floating hotel with a length of two New York City blocks and a width of about half a block'. All this had to be achieved on a maximum draught of 15 feet. The hotel had to proceed at a reasonably fast speed, that is over twenty miles an hour, and be highly manoeuverable. Above all, she had to be able to stop quickly in emergency because of the danger of collision in crowded waterways. To meet the requirements, the side paddler with her immense beam, high degree of control and freedom from vibration was very suitable in an era of relatively cheap solid fuel. The American short sea and river steamers kept to the tradition of the great central hall with gallery around it and state rooms opening off on either side. A fine example from the end of the century is among the illustrations at the end of this chapter (Plate 74).

European short sea route steamers rarely reached the degree of opulence of those of the United States and Canada but in the last thirty years of the nineteenth century they too greatly improved in speed and comfort. There is at least one vessel still in passenger service whose origins span this period. She is the paddle steamer *Skibladmer* of Eidsvoll, Norway, built in 1856 and rebuilt in 1888, still in passenger service on Lake Mjosa. Originally equipped for 150 passengers, with first and second class cabins and a library, she also had four guns. The guns have gone but the vessel still has her 1888 engine and boilers and is now able to carry 300 passengers.

The standard set on the North Atlantic route after 1870 duly affected the near Continental and coastal packets of the British Isles. The process was further encouraged by competition between the various companies and by the high standards sometimes set by the railway packet as the railway companies obtained parliamentary sanction to enter the ship-owning business. The bulk of the accommodation began to be constructed amidships or forward of the engines, forced ventilation, electric light, two-berth cabins, running hot and cold water and adequate sanitation, all followed in due course, as did also the provision of a high standard of luxury in the public apartments, even though the passengers were to be on board for at the most a couple of days and nights.

London and Calstock, 1970–1.

LIST OF PLATES

BEFORE THE NINETEENTH
CENTURY

PLATE 1

In 1962 a group of five vessels of the Viking period was salved from the bottom of the Roskilde fiord in Denmark. These included two longships, vessels generally of the type represented in the Bayeaux tapestry, cousins of the great vessel known as the Gokstad ship which is preserved at Bygdøy near Oslo and which has come to be regarded popularly as the representative 'Viking ship'. The third boat was a small or medium-sized cargo vessel, the fourth was probably a ferry or a fishing boat.

The fifth vessel, usually referred to as Skuldelev 1, is a big beamy cargo vessel with high sides, capable, given a skilful crew with sufficient hardihood, of making colonising voyages to Ireland, Greenland and North America. This vessel appears to be the first discovered example of the *knarr*, the vessels referred to in the Sagas in which the Vikings made their great trading and settling voyages.

The evidence, including that provided by Carbon 14 tests, indicates that these vessels date from the first half of the eleventh century.

The photograph shows Skuldelev 1 being rebuilt in the new Viking Ship Museum at Roskilde. She is revealed as a beamy, powerful, rather flat-floored boat of very pleasing shape. Into this boat and larger vessels of similar general form were packed men, women, children and animals for voyages across the northern part of the North Atlantic between Norway and Iceland and on to Greenland.

This was sea travel at its most rugged.

As recently as October 1970 a great open boat of similar size was discovered in the Graveney Marshes in Kent. She is now undergoing prolonged investigation and conservation at the National Maritime Museum. Dating from at least a century before Skuldelev 1, she may be the first discovered example of a British cargo and passenger vessel of the Viking period.

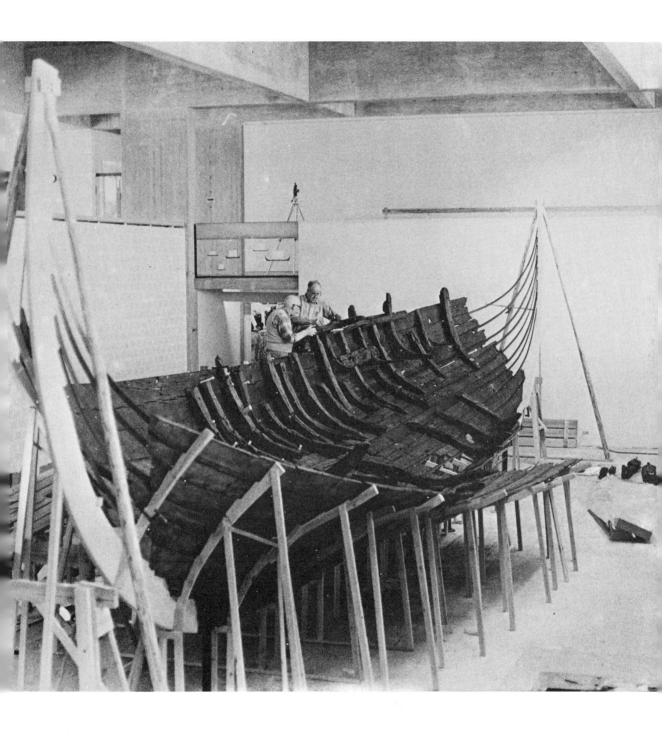

PLATE 2

When the Swedish warship *Wasa* of 1628 was raised to the surface of Stockholm harbour in 1961 the scientific excavation of her mud-filled interior began at once. The vast quantities of deposited clay and silt totalling 700 tons made the process very difficult. All this had to be washed away slowly with jets from hoses and at the same time thoroughly examined for artefacts. In this photograph the work is going forward on the lower gun-deck. Gun carriages can be seen on the left from which the guns had been moved by the remarkable efforts of seventeenth-century divers. The low and narrow environment in which the crew and passengers of even a very large early seventeenth-century vessel lived is being revealed. The orlop deck next below, where some of the petty officers had their accommodation is markedly lower still. The great cabin in the stern on the upper gun deck had about the same amount of head room as is shown in the photograph.

In this dark world of massive woodwork lived the people of a ship of the time of King Charles I of Britain, eight years after the Pilgrim Fathers sailed. The *Mayflower* herself was, of course, a much smaller vessel, though of not disimilar general shape, and her intermediate deck must have looked very similar to this space, though even more confined. It can be imagined filled with people with their chests and bundles, each having little more space than he or she took when lying down.

PLATE 3

The Quayles of Castletown, Isle of Man, were a prosperous land-owning and industrial family. Like many of their contemporaries they owned a small fleet of sailing and rowing boats which were operated jointly with local fishermen and used as workboats and as ferries to the mainland. They appear on occasion also to have been used for recreation, but they were expected to show returns for the investment made in them and they were one of the family's main means of communication with the rest of the United Kingdom.

One of these boats, the *Peggy*, built in 1791, is shown here as she lies today in the Nautical Museum at Castletown. She is 26 feet long, was propelled by six oars working in oar ports and rigged as a 'two-mast boat', that is, as a kind of small schooner. In their boats the Quayle family carried not only themselves and items purchased in Liverpool which were needed for their establishment in the Island, but also on one occasion at least a dismantled phaeton was taken to Liverpool. On another, in 1796, George Quayle, then head of the family, took the *Peggy* across to the north Lancashire coast from where she was trailed behind horses to Windermere to race with local boats on the lake.

PLATE 4

No eighteenth-century merchant ship survives to show what the accommodation of travellers was like when for the first time sea voyages were becoming a less rare experience for the ordinary man and pictures are few because cabins and intermediate decks were commonplace and did not attract artists. Few seamen or passengers sketched or painted. Those who did, did not often choose their accommodation as a subject.

However, a very good impression of the great cabin of an eighteenth-century merchant ship of 200 or 300 tons is conveyed by the contemporary replica shown in this photograph. This 'stern cabin' was built on land in 1791 by the same George Quayle who sailed the *Peggy* over to Windermere in 1796 and it is still in existence. In a fragment of a letter which appears to have been written in 1791 and which survives in the Quayle Papers in the Manx Museum, this extraordinary room is described as follows:

'The boathouse is growing apace, & we expect to make trial of the young Neptune on Easter Monday the house will be so constructed as to make room for both boats & the apartment over it will be quite an oddity, the interior alterations ornaments and Decorations are not to be described to the Vulgar until finished and even then to be seen only by the elect.'

The elect were to see a room built as a close copy of the stern cabin of what was then a medium-sized merchant vessel, complete with sloping windows and rudder trunk, cambered ceiling and a double sloping sill. It was in accommodation of this kind, about this size but perhaps divided into two or three and temporarily equipped with a few small items of their own furniture, that many hundreds of better off people travelled to North America from Britain in the late eighteenth and early nineteenth centuries.

ACCOMMODATION IN WOODEN
SAILING SHIPS

PLATE 5

This engraving by G. Humphrey after a drawing by G. Cruikshank, published in 1818, is entitled 'An interesting scene on board an East Indiaman, showing the Effects of a heavy Lurch after dinner'.

The captain's dining table runs athwartships, there are six large stern windows and glazed gun ports. The diners share the accommodation with two guns (which even as late as this date may still be needed for defensive purposes against pirates), the ramrods and powder horns stowed in the deck head, and the shot. There is nothing peculiarly maritime about the furniture. The chairs are not secured to the deck with lanyards and no fiddle grating has been fitted to the table.

Everybody is properly dressed for the main meal of the day but as this takes place in the afternoon children are present, though not at the table. Only the captain seems unperturbed. The artist has enjoyed himself depicting a formal gathering at the moment of its destruction.

The scene is not exaggerated, Robert Ramsay wrote in 1826:

'The scenes at the cuddy table baffle my powers of description: eat and drink while you can is the only way to get on; to have one hand at liberty for a whole minute was a rare occurrence. Legs of Mutton, Pork, Hams, Potatoes and etc., had no idea of remaining on their dishes. The tablecloth was dyed with soup, butter, mustard, wine, beer, and etc., and the clothes of many shared the same fate. The chairs were very fond of skating, making their owners measure their length upon the floor. Mr C's split Dr Harrison's door with his head, but for further particulars see the numerous prints entitled, "An E. Indiaman off the Cape". I had no conception these prints were so correctly done beforehand!'

ittle Cabin with 2 hamocks.

The Ship's Steward.

PLATE 6

These two little engravings were published by Longmans & Co. of Paternoster Row on 1st September 1805. They show the cabin accommodation of a large merchant ship, probably an East Indiaman. It is simple in the extreme. One engraving shows two curtained bunks, misnamed 'hamocks', in a space about twice their width. The other shows something slightly more sophisticated, a single berth with fitted drawers underneath and steps to enter it like those of a mounting block. A conspicuous feature of both cabins is the very necessary chamber pot.

The second sketch is of particular interest because it shows the contemporary dress of a passenger ship steward. He wears a loose shirt with a neckerchief, a short jacket, baggy trousers and a woollen cap. There is little to distinguish him from the seamen on deck, except that he was probably able to keep himself cleaner.

Many cabins of the period were larger than these and able to take the sort of items of passengers' furniture which have been described in the text. But considering the profit to be made from stowing eastern products for sale in England into these spaces, it is no wonder that on the homeward passage accommodation was very expensive and most people tended to travel simply.

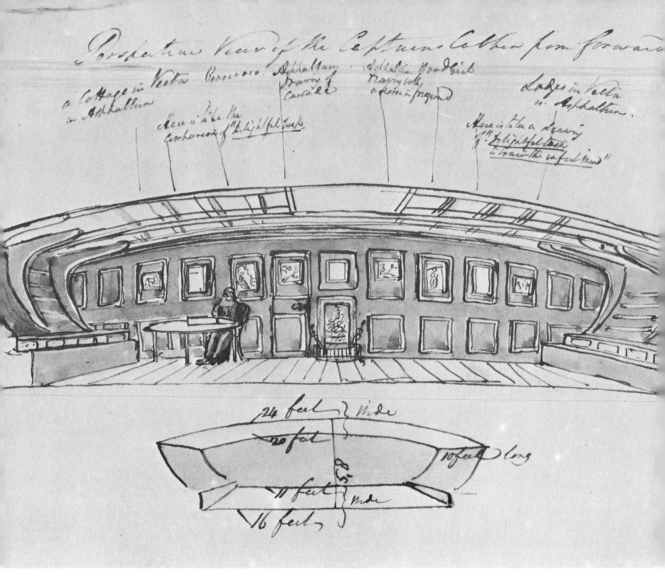

PLATE 7

The brig *St Clio* was built in 1811. Her captain, William Farrington, during the first two years of her life kept a sketch book which is now in the Peabody Museum at Salem. This photographic copy of one of the pages shows his rendering of the stern cabin. He notes each picture, and those he intends to put up in due course. He gives the dimensions of the cabin and it is apparent that in the main sketch he has exaggerated the width of the apartment by a factor of two. The cabin in real life would appear much narrower than this although the depth and general shape are right. The bulging sides are represented outside by the quarter galleries of a vessel of this period. Note the simplicity of the furnishings, one table, which was all there was really room for, side benches and a simple firegrate.

PLATE 8

In order to appreciate the conditions under which most people travelled by sea in the first half of the nineteenth century, it is necessary to look at the outside of the vessels as well as at their interiors. The *Countess of Bective*, shown left of centre in a photograph taken in the 1840s was built at Sunderland in 1843 and was engaged for many years in trade to South America. Small as she seems she is a typical merchant sailing vessel of the period 1820–50 and is in fact far more representative of the British merchant sailing ship in history than were the great steel barks of the end of the century which are often now taken as typical. The great majority of people who travelled overseas to North America, Australia, New Zealand and the Cape of Good Hope before 1860, did so in the after cabins or the 'tween decks of vessels like the *Countess of Bective*.

The limited living space such a vessel afforded can well be appreciated from this photograph, as can her basic characteristics, a flat bottom to enable her to sit upright at low tide, windows which lit the great cabin in her square stern, a very full hull (which meant that her effective speed was limited to a few miles an hour) and her rigging both complex and frail. Much of the upper parts of the rigging was dismantled in bad weather by her highly-skilled crew and sent down on deck. In this photograph the vessel lying against the quay wall has had much of the rigging and structure of her main and foremasts sent down by her crew, not because she has been excessively damaged, but for ordinary maintenance purposes.

Both vessels have gunports painted on their sides. This conventional decoration, a legacy of the Napoleonic wars, lasted until well into the twentieth century as a form of adornment for sailing vessels of all sizes.

PLATE 9

This photograph, taken at Plymouth in the 1840s, has been included because it shows the extremely simple and limited deck space available in a medium-sized merchant vessel of the period. This full-rigged ship lying wrecked in Plymouth Sound, was about 300 tons. On decks as small as these in the 1820s and 30s as many as 200 people sometimes had to find such recreation space as they could. Note the extremely small hatchways which in the early part of the century provided the only natural light and ventilation in the 'tween decks. The accommodation for the crew must have been very similar to that of the vessel of 1834 described in the text, the forecastle unlighted, unventilated, unheated and totally unfurnished.

PLATE 10

This sketch made on board the *Charlotte Jane* on her way towards Christchurch, New Zealand, in 1850 shows a vessel nearly twice as big as those illustrated in the last two pictures. But again, the deck spaces are very limited. Notice the crates to carry livestock, not only for use on the voyage but also to stock the farms of New Zealand. The sketch was made from a boat carried outboard on the vessel's port quarter.

PLAN

of the Accommodations of the fine Passenger Ship,

CHARLOTTE JANE.

730 TONS, N.M.

Alexander Lawrence, Commander,

Lying in the East India Docks,

Chartered by the Association for founding the Settlement of Canterbury in New Zealand.

To sail the 29th Augt. next, to call at Plymouth.

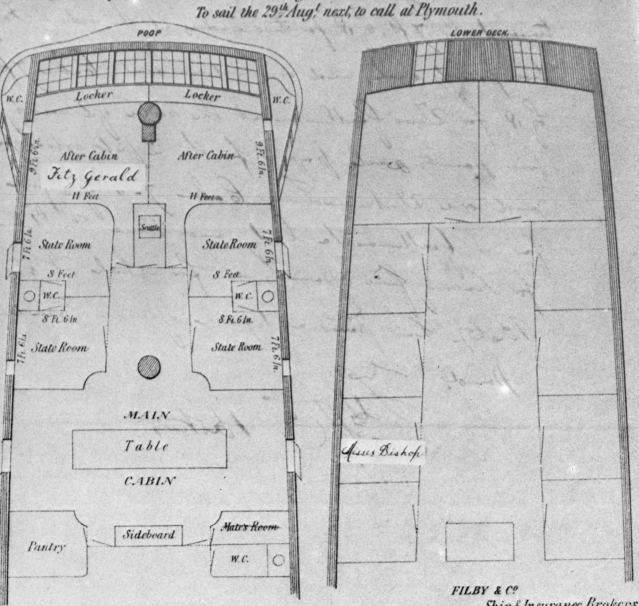

POOP

LOWER DECK

W.C.   Locker   Locker   W.C.

9 Ft. 6 in.

After Cabin   After Cabin

Fitz Gerald

11 Feet   11 Feet

7 Ft. 6 in.   State Room   Scuttle   State Room   7 Ft. 6 in.

8 Feet   8 Feet

W.C.   W.C.

8 Ft. 6 In.   8 Ft. 6 In.

7 Ft. 6 in.   State Room   State Room   7 Ft. 6 In.

MAIN

Table

CABIN

Pantry   Sideboard   Mate's Room

W.C.

Misses Bishop

FILBY & Cº

Ship & Insurance Brokers,

157, Fenchurch St.

PLATE 11

Under the poop deck of the *Charlotte Jane*, the deck in the foreground of the sketch in the last illustration, was the best passenger accommodation in the vessel. This plan shows its lay-out and the great cabin in the extreme stern with its windows and the quarter galleries divided into two spaces each measuring 11 by 9 feet and fitted as first-class double cabins. Each had three stern windows and a private lavatory in the quarter gallery. These so-called water closets were in fact probably no more than seats with holes opening straight down on to the sea below, possibly fitted with a leather flap arrangement to lessen the likelihood of a wet behind from water thrown up by the vessel's wake in bad weather, but they were a tremendous boon, particularly to women travellers. Smaller staterooms in pairs on either side immediately forward of the relatively luxurious main cabins also had their private closets but these had to be shared by the passengers in both cabins.

PLATE 12

James Fitzgerald, one of the two occupants of the starboard after cabin of the *Charlotte Jane* on her way towards New Zealand in 1850 drew this sketch of the space he shared with his wife Fanny. Very few representations are known to exist of passenger accommodation in merchant sailing ships of the first half of the century and this sketch is the more valuable because of the care with which it was executed. James Fitzgerald sat on the end of the double bed and was up against the forward bulkhead when he made it. The bed occupied six feet in front of him, then there were three feet of space, occupied mainly by their wood-and-basket-work easy chair. The stern lockers with steeply sloping stern windows above and shelves upon which a book could lie, completed the view. On the starboard side was a large basket-work trunk, a high desk and a small sofa. Lighting was by gimballed candle (there are examples of such fittings in the National Maritime Museum). The stern windows were a great comfort in the tropics. In the South Atlantic where James made his sketch, the wild, wild sea was very much apparent outside them. For weeks on end in the North Atlantic and the Southern Ocean they would have to be barricaded—'having the deadlights up' as it was termed—and during such periods the only natural light would come in through small deck lights if there were any. None are shown in the drawing.

It is important in understanding the history of travel by sea to realise that at the time this sketch was made in 1850, before the effects of the Australian gold rush had made themselves felt, the tiny cabin depicted here represented the most comfortable and expensive way of travelling for the three or four months to Australia or New Zealand from Britain and that almost all accommodation offered for passengers at least before 1850 was inferior to this.

PLATE 13

The splendid Canterbury Museum at Christchurch, New Zealand, has attempted a partial reconstruction of James and Fanny Fitzgerald's cabin. The reconstruction does not pretend to be completely realistic. There is no bed, the deckhead is two feet too high and the stern windows do not slope sufficiently. These changes in dimensions, while making it possible to display more furniture, mean that something of the claustrophobic pokiness of the original cabin is lost. But the diorama does give an impression of the best conditions at sea in the 1850s and its particular interest lies in the fact that all the items of furniture in it were carried out to New Zealand in wooden sailing ships. The two sofas, the great leather trunk, the chairs, the chest of drawers, the hat box, the china washbowl, the folding writing desk, the gimballed candlesticks, the telescope, the chessmen, are among the few artifacts on display anywhere in the world not only known to have been in their time part of the furnishings of different wooden passenger-carrying sailing ships but in most cases known to have been carried in named vessels in certain years.

PLATE 14

By way of contrast with the pictures in the preceding pages this contemporary drawing shows something of the conditions in which the great majority of passengers travelled in the early 1850s. These roughly nailed up partitions in the corner of the not very crowded 'tween decks in a wooden sailing ship remind one of nothing so much as the stables of an old country house. The rough, trough-like tables are for eating. The barrels are more likely to be for stores than part of the jealously guarded water ration. The only light comes from hanging oil lamps. There is no finish to anything or any sign of paint, everything is rough and temporary. In this space, on the next leg of the vessel's voyage will be carried part of a bulk cargo, probably of timber. Only the massive deck beams and the turned pillars have any air of permanence about them. The doorways lead into the communal dormitories where the people spend most of their time. A kind-hearted mate explains the vessel's course to an elderly, respectable peasant woman. Most of her fellow voyagers probably had little idea of where they were for most of the passage.

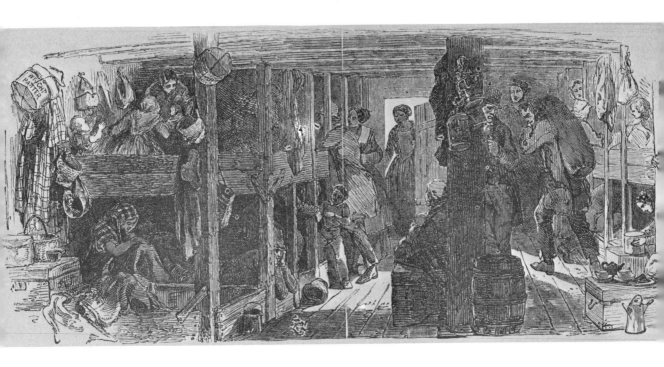

PLATE 15

This drawing from the *Illustrated London News* of 10th May, 1851, accords so closely to contemporary descriptions and has so many small touches of reality that it is generally assumed to have been drawn on the spot from life. The berths are two deep, not three as they were in similar circumstances in some earlier vessels. They are virtually the living places as well as the sleeping places of the people whose possessions are limited to their clothes and a few cooking utensils. There is of course no furniture. The rough temporary construction of the berths, nailed together from soft-wood, is very obvious. They are double box berths in which children play, women sew, men gossip. The equipment for brewing tea is visible on top of a travelling chest. Clothes, hats, hat-boxes, baskets, hang from the bulkheads and pillars. At least two babies are visible. The smell of crowded, unwashed humanity must have been appalling. There was, of course, no privacy of any kind.

PLATE 16

This picture is entitled 'turning in' and it illustrates the problem of going to bed in the best accommodation in a vessel bound from Portsmouth to Lisbon in 1831. It was sketched by Robert Seymour, engraved by Thomas M'Lean and published by C. Motte, Leicester Square. Again the furniture is simple in the extreme and apart from the cot nothing about it is especially maritime. The scene is the stern cabin and the cot presents an almost insuperable problem.

PLATE 17

Published in June 1824, this etching illustrates the arrangements in the best passenger accommodation in the contemporary short voyage packet ship. The central great cabin has two tiers of comfortable double berths on each side. Food is served at a central table and there is no segregation of the sexes. The compartment resembles the sleeping accommodation in some types of American trains fifty years later. The passengers are prosperous and well-dressed and the emphasis is on their humiliation and discomforture by seasickness and by the difficulty of remaining upright because of the violent motion of the vessel. The majority cannot enjoy their food. Those who can, and there is plenty of it available, are in the process of losing it because the motion of the vessel is throwing it off the table. Food and food regurgitated mingle on the floor in squalor. Some less (or perhaps really more) fortunate passengers huddle under umbrellas on deck.

PLATE 18

This sketch published in 1814 shows conditions rather similar to those illustrated on the proceeding page but in a smaller vessel. Again, contemporary humour draws its laughter from the contrast between rich food uneaten and squandered on the floor and seasickness. There is a steward in attendance in a hat not unlike that illustrated in Plate 6.

PLATE 19

This drawing in the National Maritime Museum, the origin of which is unknown, shows the accommodation under the poop deck of a large Atlantic packet vessel, probably American. The staterooms open on to a long, narrow central saloon, equipped with a long table with benches, one section of which has a fixed back. Here the passengers eat. Amidships is a great urn of water with a supply of glasses. The whole is lit by a central skylight. This is the principal recreation area of the passengers below decks and here a number of them are shown gossiping and reading.

PLATE 20

This drawing by R. C. Leslie was made in the 1880s but records memories of his youth in the 1840s when he crossed the Atlantic in passenger ships four times. The picture is full of incident. The cooper is making a barrel, assisted by a boy. A couple, the woman nursing a baby, sit on a spare spar lashed down on deck. Two seamen in their watch below are playing cards on top of the boxed-in boat which has been equipped to take two tiers of poultry coops. The boat is lashed down on the forehatch. Immediately aft a cow stands in the stall. She provides milk for the cabin passengers. On top of the cow's stall a young woman sits and knits. Two seamen are using a simple rope-making machine. Forward is the galley, the main source of cooked food for 'tween decks passengers and crew. More card playing is going on on the forecastle head. The foremast is composite, made up of several pieces of timber bound together with iron bands like the foremast fitted to the *Great Britain* in 1853, which can now be seen at the National Maritime Museum. The natural fibre rope standing rigging is massively thick.

93

PLATE 21

Here R. C. Leslie, drawing on his recollections of passages in this class of vessel, shows men and women cooking their rations in pots hanging on a bar above a long iron brazier immediately forward of the galley, the opening sliding door of which (with cat curled contentedly above) can be seen on the righthand side of the drawing. Note the washing hanging on a line, slung from the mainstay, the potatoes in a shallow tub, the poultry from the ship's livestock, freshly killed for cabin passengers, hanging inside and outside the galley.

PLATE 22

The *Charles W. Morgan* was built in 1841 at Fairhaven near New Bedford, Massachusetts. She was built for the old whaling trade, the hunting of sperm whales from small boats on voyages lasting often for several years. The *Morgan* made thirty-seven long voyages and was at sea for no less than eighty years before she was preserved as a monument of mid-nineteenth-century maritime technology in general and the old sailing whaling industry—which played a significant part in American economic development—in particular. Today she lies at Mystic, Connecticut, the prized principal exhibit of the maritime museum there, the world's oldest large merchant ship, the only survivor of the wooden sailing vessels which have been the subject of this chapter. In her alone it is possible to see at first hand the accommodation and ship's furniture of the period as it really was. This first photograph shows the stern cabin with four shallow stern windows separated by the rudder trunk amidships, a row of convenient drawers, a great sofa stuffed with horsehair and the doorways leading to the small cabins of the master and mate on either side. The arrangement, varying in detail, is in general similar to that illustrated in Plates 4 and 12.

PLATE 23

In this simple white walled room the master of an average-sized merchant ship of the 1840s passed his sleeping hours. The bed might well have been on land, it is a massively made ordinary big bed of the period. The wash-bowl rests on the stand in the foreground on the right. The only other furniture is the captain's sea-chest, his bookshelf, a spittoon and the important tell-tale compass hanging in a gimbal mounting above the bed.

PLATE 24

The amidships main cabin in the *Charles W. Morgan* looking forward shows the mizzen mast rising through the small dining table fitted with its gratings and with the heavy china laid out for a meal. Here, as the label puts it, the captain and his five mates dined, they were served by the steward from the pantry on the starboard side forward.

PLATE 25

This photograph taken on board the *Charles W. Morgan* gives an indication of what the closets referred to in contemporary accounts of voyages and which appear on plans of accommodation, actually looked like. The closet attached to Fanny and James Fitzgerald's cabin in the *Charlotte Jane* (Plates 11 and 12), probably had a window but otherwise must have appeared very much like this.

PLATE 26

The bark *Guy C. Goss* was built at Bath, Maine, in 1879 and is said at one time to have been the largest bark-rigged wooden vessel under the flag of the United States. The photograph shows the tremendous advances in standards of accommodation which took place in the second half of the nineteenth-century. In comparison with the rugged simplicity of the *Charles W. Morgan*, the *Guy C. Goss*, not a passenger-carrying vessel but an ordinary merchantman, gave her captain and mates very comfortable quarters. The main cabin with its organ, panelling, carved pilasters and deep padded furniture reflects all the luxury of a prosperous nineteenth-century New England home.

PLATE 27

The *Josephus* was built at Newcastle, Maine, in 1876. Her cabin shows the usual prosperity of New England vessels of this period when the grain trade from San Francisco to Europe was providing lucrative cargoes for many big wooden New England sailing vessels. The deck head is high, there is a piano in place of the organ, and the furniture generally is that of a middle-income Maine home of the period. The bowler-hatted master and his young wife have posed for the photographer.

PLATE 28

This photograph, taken in 1939 by one of the authors, gives some impression of the little saloon with small cabins opening off it of a 200-ton barkentine of a type built for general ocean trade. The *Frances & Jane* was built in Harwich in 1878. Her voyages have not been checked but she is said by one authority to have been employed in the Newfoundland trade from Britain. Certainly vessels of her type sailed all over the world in the last decades of the nineteenth century and the small cabins and central saloon were the homes for months on end of a master and two mates. At the time the photograph was taken the vessel had been laid up for many years and she was broken up during World War II. As far as is known this is the only photograph to survive of the accommodation in a wooden sailing ship of this type.

PLATE 29

The wooden three-masted schooner *Kathleen & May* was built at Connah's Quay, Flintshire, in 1900 and she has survived to the present day. Typical of many hundreds of vessels of the same period and earlier which were built for the trade to Newfoundland from Europe with salt and general cargo, returning with salted fish, interspersed with shorter voyages around the British coast and to North European ports and the Mediterranean, the *Kathleen & May*, now preserved by the Maritime Trust in most appropriate surroundings at Sutton Harbour, Plymouth, is the last surviving small British wooden merchant sailing ship not altered entirely from her original form. This photograph shows the after cabin in which the master spent much of his life when he was not on deck and in which all the crew except the man at the wheel ate together—for these schooners were democratic vessels—served often by the youngest member, who ate last.

PLATE 30

The simplicity of the accommodation provided for the crew of a small wooden sailing vessel is well illustrated by this modern photograph of the forecastle of the *Kathleen & May*. This was a below decks forecastle in which four men lived. The Atlantic voyages in which vessels of this class (though not the *Kathleen & May* herself) were employed from Britain sometimes lasted for eight weeks during which the crew had only this small forecastle in which to spend all their leisure hours.

The below decks forecastles of the nineteenth century such as that of the *Kathleen & May* provided such poor accommodation for seamen that many vessels, particularly from the United States, Canada and Scandinavia were built with deckhouse accommodation for the crews. This photograph shows the deckhouse of the barentine *Hoppet*, built in 1878, but the deckhouse forecastle of the *Pride of Wales* (see Chapter Two) must have looked very much like this. The accommodation, although by no means luxurious, is markedly better than that of the *Kathleen & May*, especially bearing in mind that it was far less likely to get flooded or to be the subject of persistent leaks than the below decks forecastles. The motion was less violent because the deckhouse was situated away from the extreme end of the vessel and access was much easier, particularly in bad weather. The *Hoppet* herself was Swedish, but this accommodation could equally well have been found in a United States or Canadian schooner or barentine and in some British vessels of the late nineteenth century.

PLATE 32

The *Glencoe* was built at Borstal in 1905. She was a typical London river sailing barge of her period. Her crew of two lived aft in berths on each side of the cabin, shown here looking forward, in what were for their time quite good conditions. The degree of comfort depended on what the men made of their opportunities. The *Glencoe* was made into a houseboat some years ago and this accommodation was stripped and rebuilt in the National Maritime Museum, where it is now possible for visitors to see how the men of one of the last types of wooden sailing ships lived at the very end of the nineteenth century.

PLATE 33

The tiny cabin of this North Sea fishing ketch has a folding table, lockers and bunks let into the cabin walls above them. The beams are little more than five feet above the deck and the space is extremely cramped and fitted into the narrowing shape of the vessel in the stern. Life in the thousands of small wooden sailing ships of this kind was rough in the extreme.

IRON AND STEEL SHIPS
AS PASSENGER CARRIERS

PLATE 34

A young couple, possibly honeymooners, relax on deck on board the *Macquarie*, a full-rigged ship in the Australian trade in the 1890s. She sits in front of one of the cabin skylights, he in the inevitable basket chair. A brass binnacle and the handles of a pump can be seen.

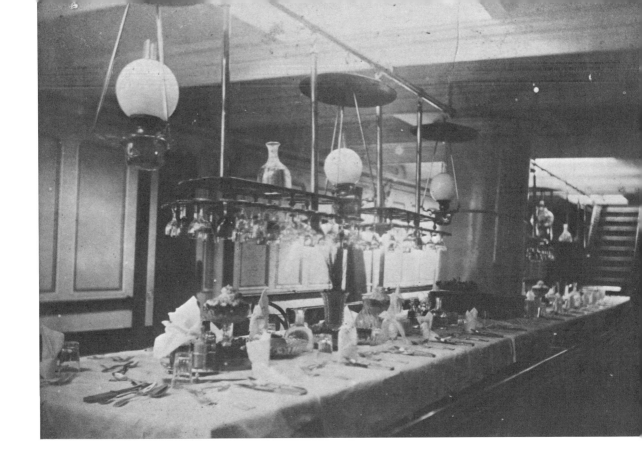

PLATE 35

The *Macquarie* had excellent accommodation under her long poop. In the long main saloon was a communal central table, pierced by the mizzen mast. Over the table hung oil lamps and racks, or swinging fiddles, of wine glasses slung upside down to keep them safe in any weather. In this photograph the table is laid for the midday meal. The menu, although necessarily repetitive, would be as attractive as it was possible to make it, given the facilities for the preservation of food of the 1890s.

This main saloon was not used only for eating, like a modern passenger ship's restaurant. It also served as a lounge, writing room, occasionally as a concert hall, in fact for every activity which could not be performed on deck or in the passengers' cabins.

PLATE 36

This photograph shows the master's saloon in a British iron or steel merchant sailing ship of the late nineteenth century. It is evident that the master works at the table because his massive inkwell is standing on it as well as his bell for calling the steward. Heating is by coal stove and the cabin is brightly lit in the daytime with a big skylight, less brightly at night with a single swinging oil lamp. The cabin is not in a deckhouse, but under the poop, possibly almost in the stern of the vessel. There is the usual organ and a plush-topped stool to play it from. The door out into the alleyway is discreetly curtained. By the standards of the times this is comfortable middle-class accommodation.

PLATE 37

The *Olivebank* was built in Glasgow in 1892. This unusual photograph of the watch below was taken inside her forecastle in the 1930s, when she was still earning her living at sea under the Finnish flag. Little has been changed since she was built and the photograph shows well the simplicity of the accommodation and of the furnishings. This is a topgallant forecastle, that is, a compartment right in the very eyes of the vessel, under the capstan on the forecastle head, the traditional place for the crews' quarters in a large sailing vessel. One man is doing some fancy rope work, another is sewing, two play chess, one plays a fiddle and another a concertina. The picture is quite unposed. The slope of the kettle reveals that the vessel was on the port tack when the photograph was taken.

113

PLATE 38

The *Falls of Clyde*, an iron four-masted full-rigged ship of 1,800 tons, was built in 1878 by Russell & Co., Port Glasgow, for Wright, Breakenridge and Co., Ltd of Glasgow. She was a sailing tramp and in this role she made seven circumnavigations in the next eighteen years. In 1898 she was sold to American owners who refitted her as a four-masted bark with passenger accommodation in the poop for the trade between Hawaii and San Francisco. In this trade she made over sixty passages in eight years. She then became a bulk oil tanker and made many more passages including two round voyages to Europe as late as the 1920s.

The *Falls of Clyde* is now being restored at Honolulu to her working and sailing appearance as part of the famous B.P. Bishop Museum. This photograph shows her saloon as it was in her passenger-carrying days with staterooms opening off on either side.

PLATE 39

When the *Falls of Clyde* came under United States ownership her topgallant forecastle was replaced as the crew's accommodation by a deckhouse forecastle, a process which occurred in many sailing vessels in the late nineteenth century—see the last chapter. It is this relatively comfortable deckhouse forecastle which is shown here. Compared with the topgallant fore-castles which were right in the bows, shared with the windlass and chain hawser, and with bare steel walls, this is almost luxurious. Moreover, it is situated in a dry part of the vessel with the galley adjacent to it—a great convenience which meant the watch below could usually count on hot food and drink at regular hours.

ACCOMMODATION IN EARLY STEAMERS

An American Steam Vessel.

Published at R. Ackermann's, 101 Strand, May 1.

View of British Steam Vessels

Under-Weigh, as Designed, and Constructed by Barrodall Robt. Dodd,

Civil Engineer of *Newcastle on Tyne.*

'Soon shall thy arm, unconquered steam! afar
Force the swift barge, or drive the rapid car.'

Or on wide waving wings expanded bear
The flying chariot through the fields of air'. *Darwin.*

Interior of the Principal Cabin.

PLATE 40

This very early representation of a British steam vessel was published by R. Ackermann at 101 Strand on 1st May 1817. It shows on the left 'an American steam vessel', and on the right a grossly over-crowded steamer with a squaresail set from her funnel to aid her engine, a device apparently often used in early steam vessels. In the centre is a contemporary Newcastle-on-Tyne-built steamer, again grossly over-crowded by later standards. Her accommodation is evidently concentrated into two cabins fore and aft of the engine compartment and what appears to be the after cabin is illustrated in the next plate.

PLATE 41

This charming little sketch is almost certainly the earliest representation of the accommodation in a British steam vessel which exists. It shows an elegant Regency-style apartment with carpeted floor and curtained windows, and passengers seated on the benches at the sides of the cabin which were to remain a feature of the accommodation of the steam packets for many years. They are entertaining themselves with conversation, games and wine-drinking. The ceiling is particularly elaborate and the dome roof light corresponds to the circular seat on the after deck in the proceeding plate.

On His Most Gracious Majesty
KING GEORGE THE FOURTH,
The Illustrious Patron of Steam Packets,
This Plate is dedicated by
His Majesty's most devoted
and faithful Servant Subject
John Hudson

PLATE 42

The *Victory*, Captain Corbin, was built at Rotherhithe under the direction of Captain George Dodd who commanded the *Thames* on her historic voyage from the Clyde to London in 1815. This acquatint was published by John Hudson, 85 Cheapside, on 5th September 1821. It shows two views of the *Victory* off Margate with two of her rival sailing packets in the London-Margate trade in the background, both, no doubt deliberately, shown becalmed. The *Victory's* main cabins are the full width of the vessel, lit with square ports on either side. The plate is inscribed that the *Victory* was:

'built under the direction of George Dodd, Esq., Civil Engineer, the Founder of the Steam Packets to Margate, Gravesend and Richmond and who commanded the first Steam Yacht which crofsed the Irish Channel and entered Dublin Harbour'.

PLATES 43 and 44

These two views of the *Victory's* fore and after cabins could not be finer illustrations of the contemporary best interpretation of the accommodation in one of the earliest steam packets. The dresses and decorations are splendid, as is also the food and the general air of luxury. As in a modern travel brochure, everyone is prosperous and of assured social position. But the details, the steps up into the stern, the stern windows, the arched deckhead, the spacing of the window ports, are all correct. And the fare, even from London to Margate was high enough to ensure that at least in the cabin it was a journey only for the well-to-do. It is a pity Jane Austen did not live to make it and give us an account.

PLATE 45

This view of steamers at St Louis, Missouri, shows ordinary work-a-day American river vessels. These are not smart, gaily painted craft but simply-built utilitarian scows with steam engines in them, paddle wheels and rough, solid, superstructures built of wood for carrying barrels, sacks and bales, farm carts, cattle and passengers. The decorations are mainly a little scroll-saw work of a standard type common on even quite small farmhouses in the United States and Canada in the mid-nineteenth century. These steamers operate against a background not of plantations and big houses but of industry and sordid waterfronts. Vessels very like these were still operating on the great rivers of East Pakistan a few years ago.

123

PLATE 46

The grander American river steamers had very sumptuous accommodation for passengers. The tradition of the great central compartment with the accommodation rooms built round it on two or three levels lasted into the twentieth century. This compartment was sometimes decorated with every kind of baroque magnificence and the finer and more thoroughly publicised river steamboats became legends in their own life time. This contemporary drawing shows one in the 1860s or 70s – but they changed very little between 1830 and 1914. This grand structure was, of course, a piece of stage scenery in a river boat which was lightly and flimsily built. If it caught fire the results could be dreadful.

THE PADDLE LINERS

PLATE 47

At least two versions exist of this sketch of the inside of Charles Dickens' cabin in the *Britannia*.
It is important to remember that there was no running water in the washbowls – this was
brought in jugs by a steward or stewardess. But then there was little or no running water in
any sleeping accommodation ashore in the 1840s. In almost every hotel and in all big houses
all water was carried to the bedrooms by servants. The slops drained into buckets in the
cupboards, which until their periodic emptyings must have splashed dolefully backwards
and forwards. The water closets were few and some way from the cabins so that sanitation
must have been largely by the provision of chamber pots. There is no wardrobe and passengers
were expected to live out of their trunks. In some ways this accommodation is inferior to the
two best stern cabins of the *Charlotte Jane*, but the point is that it was generally and regularly
available and not a rare luxury. The era of mass travel was at its very beginnings and, for all
Dickens' criticisms of the *Britannia*, new and higher general standards of comfort and convenience at sea were from now on increasingly and competitively introduced.

127

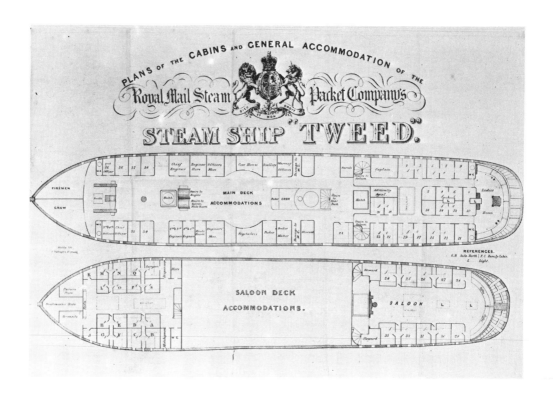

PLATE 48

The accommodation plan of the paddle steam liners discussed at length in the text is very well illustrated in this contemporary drawing of the *Tweed*, of the Royal Mail Steam Packet Company, trading to the West Indies. She was a sister ship of the *Forth*, a long quotation about conditions in which appears in the text, and like the *Britannia* she operated in the 1840s. She was built on the Clyde by Messrs Thompson and Spiers and she had accommodation for ninety-two passengers and sixty officers and men. Her side-lever engines developed 450 nominal horsepower. As can be seen, her accommodation was on two decks, the lower broken by the engine and boiler room space, the upper continuous. At the forward end of the lower deck were the little second class cabins. At the after end were the first class cabins, each leading off an alleyway, in turn this lead off the saloon which had sofas in the stern which were occasionally used as passenger overflow accommodation. There was only one lavatory on the whole of the lower deck and it is to be assumed that the majority of the passengers there used the traditional pots or commodes in the cabins (as they would have done in a house or hotel ashore). On the upper deck there are more first class cabins, some alternating with the officers' accommodation and on this deck also is the cow house and no less than six lavatories, two of them in the paddle sponsons. There was a bakery, a ladies' room in the extreme stern where, in anything of a sea, all but the most hardened female passengers must have been sick, and two forecastles, right in the eyes of the vessel for the deck hands and firemen. There were no bathrooms for anyone. The *Tweed* was built to the highest contemporary specifications but she was lost with seventy-two lives on the Alicranes reefs off Yucatan in the Gulf of Mexico in February, 1847.

128

PLATE 49

This contemporary drawing from the *Illustrated London News* shows a 'Family Cabin' in the *Great Eastern*. It represents the best standard of accommodation in this great vessel, with four curtained bunks, a comfortable sofa and a porthole. The washstand is visible just beyond the door on the left and the rocking chair must have been very awkward in anything of a sea – the *Great Eastern* could move very violently indeed under adverse conditions.

PLATE 50

This photograph was taken on board the *Great Eastern* in the 1880s when this sadly-fated vessel was fulfilling her last role as a floating exhibition. It was taken in what was originally the ladies' saloon and, although the furnishings had been much altered and the space was used as a restaurant, it still gives some idea in such details as the chandeliers, the mirrors, the pillars and pilasters and the decorations around the skylight, of the lavishness with which this, the greatest of all the paddle liners, was originally fitted out.

PLATES 51 and 52

These details from a contemporary draught in the National Maritime Museum show in unique degree parts of the accommodation in the *Persia*, almost the last of the great paddle liners. Although she was built fifteen years later, in 1855, the *Persia's* general lay-out was similar to that of the *Tweed* (Plate 48). She had passenger accommodation on two decks abaft the engine room (the parts shown here). The accommodation comprised on the lower deck two long rows of cabins, each with two bunks, one above the other, a washstand, a mirror and a sofa, on each side of the central saloon which was furnished with benches and tables. Forward was more recreation space, staircases and leather-upholstered, padded sofas. On the upper deck, in a series of houses between the very high bulwarks, was a long saloon fitted with tables and side benches, lighted with big square ports with decorated panels between them. The whole gives an impression of accommodation which would still have been very acceptable in the second class a century later.

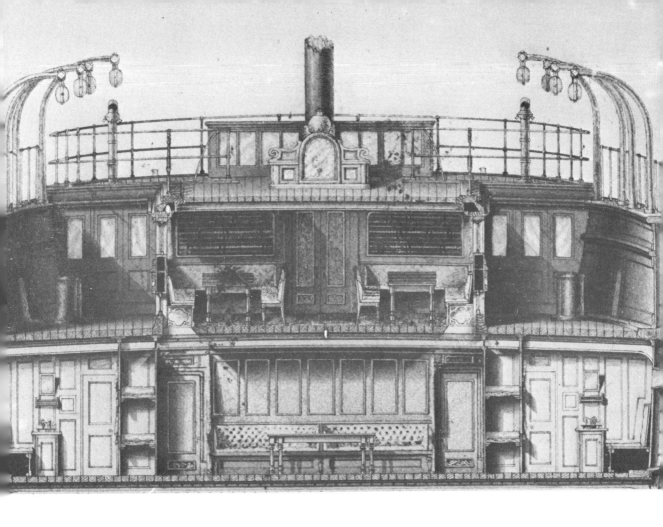

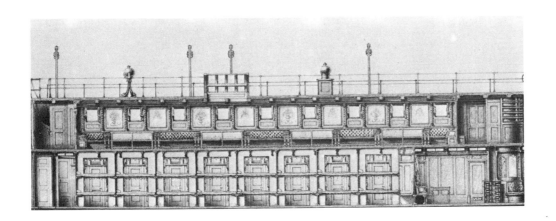

TRAVELLING PALACES

PLATE 53

This delicately-coloured water-colour drawing of 1852 in the National Maritime Museum shows the main saloon of the *Great Britain* immediately after she had been refitted as an auxiliary steamship for the Australian passenger trade. It is of particular value as an illustration of the saloon conditions which persisted until the 1860s – the eating space used as a recreation space for writing, reading, talking and drinking when meals were not being served, the hanging gratings for decanters and glasses and the reversible-backed benches referred to in the text of Chapter Five as being characteristic of the saloons of the paddle liners are particularly well illustrated. The standard of decoration and of soft furnishings appears very high and even allowing for artistic exaggeration (the deckhead, for instance, was much lower than this drawing suggests) the accommodation appears relatively spacious. One can see how the *Great Britain* established her reputation for comfort through all the changes she underwent in her long years of service.

PLATE 54

By the 1870s the upper decks of steamships had begun to resemble a train running through a cutting, the long narrow deckhouses which stretched almost from end to end of the vessel corresponded to the coaches, the high bulwarks which were sometimes as high as the deckhouses themselves were the sides of the cutting. Some first class passengers lived in these deck cabins, others of the cabins provided recreation space.

Though this pattern of accommodation changed out of all recognition in North Atlantic passenger vessels in the early 1870s, it persisted on other routes for another ten to twenty years. This photograph shows the upper deck of the *Rome*, an iron screw steamer of 5,000 tons built at Greenock in 1881 for the P. & O. London – India or Ceylon – Melbourne – Sydney service. Although the bulwarks are lower than those of some earlier vessels this photograph gives a good impression of the way in which the distribution of accommodation on the top decks of passenger steamships had developed before the revolution introduced by the *Oceanic*.

PLATE 55

On her maiden voyage the *Rome* inaugurated the use of Tilbury as the P. & O. Company's English terminus. She had accommodation for 160 first class and 60 second class passengers in quarters which were superior to those provided by any of her predecessors. The P. & O. at this time did not carry third class passengers or emigrants.

The music room of the *Rome* must have been a sombre place, despite the brilliant lighting from the skylight and the square ports, each pair separated by a carved panel with a musical motif. The room, of course, was in one of the deckhouses illustrated in the last photograph. The benches with which it was lined were upholstered in rich black leather, their heavy mahogany arms carved to a degree which must have made their practical use as armrests almost impossible. The piano, too, was so elaborately decorated that it almost must have seemed a non-functional object and the whole apartment from the plastered ceiling to the bank of ferns and the mock-Jacobean carpet must rather have absorbed than enhanced the music that came from it. Nevertheless, the music room represented another step forward in a period of very rapidly developing luxury for first class passengers at sea.

PLATE 56

The second class dining-room in the *Rome* was situated on a lower deck in the extreme stern of the vessel and the photograph shows clearly the shape of the inside of her semi-eliptical counter in which big square ports played some of the role of the stern windows of the vessels of a generation earlier. The furnishings were a great deal simpler than those in the first class. The piano had none of the heavy carving of the instrument shown in the last photograph and one can imagine some jolly thumping accompaniments producing some rousing choruses after the evening meal. Second class passengers made do with a painted iron deckhead, not for them the figured papered ceilings or the elaborately carved panels which are seen in some of the following photographs of first class accommodation. Of particular interest are the hanging punkahs, designed to ensure some movement of air during the passage of the Suez Canal and the Red Sea. Such punkahs would be very familiar to many of the passengers. Manually-operated punkahs were used throughout India, and despite the rapid development of the horizontal electric fan were still occasionally to be met with in country districts as late as the 1950s.

PLATE 57

By way of contrast this photograph of the buffet in the first class saloon of the *Rome* shows an extreme of ornate opulence. These chairs were never meant to be relaxed in, while the contrast between the scale and decoration of this 'Italianate' saloon and the conditions on board the *Britannia* less than forty years earlier is roughly equivalent to the difference between the accommodation offered by an airliner of the 1970s and the canvas seats and discomforts of the 1930s. In fact, the carvings of game birds, fish, cupids' and hound's heads, the door panels whose decorations contain the words 'Cambi', 'Siena', 'Italia', 'Toscana' like labels hung on a decanter, the crowing cock above the clock supported by *putti*, all these things were no doubt to entice and entertain the passenger as international airlines use feature films on closed-circuit television today. But there are recorded cases of first class passengers escaping from the overwhelming interiors of their own accommodation to the relative simplicity of the second class, and this photograph of the *Rome* perhaps suggests why some people felt compelled from time to time to forego the luxury they had paid for.

138

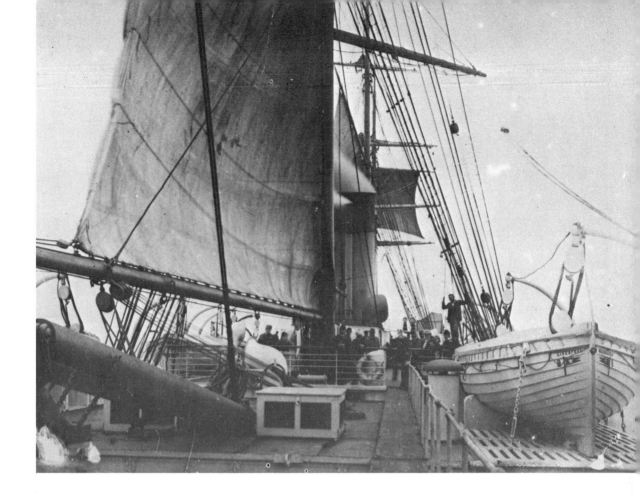

PLATE 58

The revolution introduced by the *Oceanic* meant the replacing of the narrow deckhouses and high bulwarks by a completely new deck covered over so that the covering deck itself provided yet another deck level surrounded by railings. Under this deck the first class accommodation was concentrated amidships in space which extended from one side of the vessel to the other.

This change is illustrated very vividly in this photograph taken on board the *Germanic*, built for the White Star Line in 1874, which should be compared with the view on the *Rome's* upper deck in Plate 54. The photograph also provides a rare on board impression of a steam-and-sail vessel at sea with canvas set.

The *Germanic* was the first large passenger vessel to have forced draught ventilation and thus for the first time first class passengers had some control over the temperature of their cabins and emigrants had some fresh air.

S.S. Teutonic, White Star State Room N°13ᴬ

PLATE 59

The White Star Liner *Teutonic*, built by Harland and Wolff at Belfast in 1889 was among the first twin-screw liners and was indeed built as the White Star Line's response to the innovation of twin-screws by the Inman Line. This photograph of a first class stateroom shows an extremely comfortable apartment with such novelties as a power point for a bedside light, an electric bell and a big square window in which the frosted glass carries on the design of the wall panels. Today's fashion for matched William Morris wallpapers and furnishing fabrics and Victorian brass bedsteads leads us to admire this charming room.

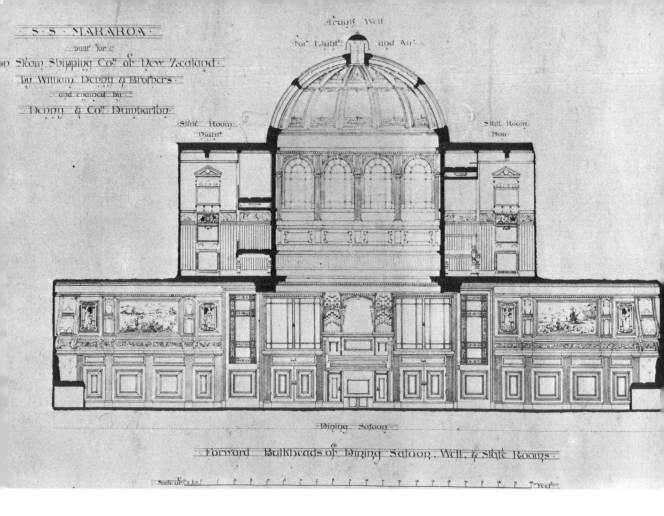

S·S· MARAROA
built for
Union Steam Shipping Co⁰ of New Zealand
by William Denny & Brothers
and engined by
Denny & Co⁰ Dumbarton

State Room
Night

State Room
Day

Trunk Well
for Light and Air

Dining Saloon

Forward Bulkheads of Dining Saloon, Well, & State Rooms

Scale of ... Feet

PLATE 60

In 1885, the old-established firm of William Denny and Company of Dumbarton built the screw-steamer *Mararoa* for the Union Steamship Company of New Zealand. She was a vessel of only 2,500 tons for the intercolonial trade between New Zealand and Australia, but William Denny's drawing shop produced elaborate designs for her accommodation, one of which is shown here. This is the forward bulkhead of the first class accommodation arranged in the after part of the vessel. It shows the decoration of the dining saloon with pilasters, a frieze, urns, landscape murals and single figures draped in classical costumes in an appropriate setting between a pair of columns. It was the fashion for these female figures to represent a series of abstract ideas – the Seasons and 'Painting', 'Architecture', 'Music' and 'Sculpture' were chosen for the *Mararoa* and as the designs were somewhat lacking in invention these titles were a necessary part of them, in this instance they were painted on the entablature above each figure. Other Denny vessels were adorned with females labelled 'Engineering', 'Billiards' and 'Medicine'.

There is an organ amidships under the trunk well which, even in this smallish vessel, is got up like a cathedral dome. On either side of the well are staterooms with double berths, one above the other. The port stateroom is shown as if at night, the starboard as for the day with the upper berth pulled up to the ceiling and the lower berth arranged as a couch. Note the tall folding washstand in each stateroom. Washstands of this kind were one of the few distinctively maritime articles of furniture to evolve. They occur in vessels of all classes and an example is shown in detail in the next photograph.

141

PLATE 61

This tall folding washstand is a typical example of one of the few units of furniture developed specifically for shipboard use. In this particular one the water appears to come from a piped supply and the bowl would have to be removed for emptying. Often copper tanks which had to be periodically refilled were concealed behind the mirror and in some washstands the bowl was simply tipped up with the folding shelf to which it was secured and the waste water ran either into a drain or into a tank below which had to be emptied daily. The lowest cupboard was for chamber pots.

Somebody in the firm of Denny & Co of Dumbarton must have been very proud of this design – the company's albums in the National Maritime Museum contain several versions of this photograph showing the washstand both open and closed.

PLATE 62

The *Scott* was built by William Denny and Co of Dumbarton for the Britain–South Africa service of the Union Line in 1890. She carried 204 first class passengers who were from time to time entertained by a performer on this piano as the vessel proceeded on her voyages at high speed – she was one of the rare instances of a vessel built for service other than on the North Atlantic in the design of which speed rather than economy of operation in relation to the service route had been the main consideration. She was the first liner on the South African route to follow the twenty year old example of the White Star Line on the North Atlantic and put the first class passengers amidships. Her passage of fourteen days, eighteen hours, fifty-seven minutes to Cape Town in 1893 established a record which stood for forty-three years.

Looking at this photograph out of its context, who would guess that it came from anywhere but the newly-built mansion of a wealthy Victorian tycoon? The piano – and the buffet – were the altars and this one is enshrined with all the trappings of material prosperity.

143

PLATE 63

The elaborate carved pillars and all the work reflected in the mirror in the last plate were made up in the woodcarver's shop at Denny's yard, shown here, probably tidied up for the photographer, with some examples of ship carver's work and patterns for a good many more. The row of framed photographs of classical sculptures and the details of bas-reliefs above the windows no doubt provided inspiration for many a tour-de-force in the first class saloons. This was a skilled trade which required years of apprenticeship to master.

PLATE 64

The *Australia* was a 7,000-ton triple-expansion compound engine screw steamer built at Greenock in 1892 for the P. & O. She lasted only twelve years, being lost by fire in 1904. She had a service speed of 18 knots and carried 251 first and 74 second class passengers. She created a record in 1893 when she steamed to Adelaide from London in 26 days, 16 hours. The photograph shows the first class smoking-room, electrically lit, with dark upholstery and wallpaper, heavy carved bench ends and tables, panelled door and square curtained windows. It is the atmosphere of a private bar ashore rather than that of a club but still very much a male preserve. The absence of a carpet suggests that beer and cigarette ash would litter the floor by the end of the day.

The *Himalaya* was built at Greenock in 1892 for the P. & O. service to Colombo, Melbourne and Sydney. She was a sister to the *Australia* and carried the same number of passengers in each class. She was commissioned as an armed merchant cruiser during World War I and broken up in 1922.

The photograph shows the music room, all white and gilt with a white-enamelled grand piano at one end, white pillars, panels and pilasters and a polished brass rail round the delicate wrought iron and brass screen guarding the central well. There is a lightness of touch and a pleasant unity in the design of this room. The electric lighting is discreet. On the lozenges above the square ports are carved the names of famous composers.

PLATE 66

There follows a series of photographs illustrative of the extreme luxury of the Victorian screw passenger steamship at its best. The *Lucania* of 13,000 tons was built by the Fairfield Ship-building Company in 1893 for Cunard in order to compete with the 10,000 ton ships such as the *Teutonic*, then being put on to the Atlantic route by the White Star Line. The *Lucania* was one of the first Cunarders not to be equipped with sails. She was also one of the first North Atlantic liners to be built with single berth cabins and with suites, that is cabins in pairs with a sitting room between them. She was the first vessel to have coal-burning firegrates in all the principal rooms. She represented a standard of opulence in the first class accommodation not reached before even in the North Atlantic service and her rooms were described as suggesting 'the stately chambers of a palace rather than accommodation within the steel walls of a ship'. Appropriately, she is believed to have been the first Cunarder in which the most expensive cabins were officially referred to as the first class and in 1903 she printed the first ship's newspaper, receiving news from Marconi stations at Poldhu and Cape Breton.

One feels that some pretty heavy books must have been digested in this library but, alas, we cannot read their titles. It is a far cry from the few good books which Charles Dickens found kept under lock and key in the *Britannia*. The walls were of carved mahogany and Amboyna panels with writing tables and chairs arranged along them. The velvet upholstery was blue.

PLATE 67

In the first class dining room of the *Lucania* the standard of opulence set by the library is maintained in what was described as 'the modified Italian style' by an even heavier coffered ceiling in white and gold supported by Ionic columns, the Spanish mahogany walls are richly carved with pilasters and other devices, there are broken pediments and clocks over all the sideboards. The room is enormous, occupying of course the whole width of the ship with seats for 430 people. The old tradition of the long dining table has not been entirely lost, even in

148

1893, but instead of one table there are at least four with numerous small side tables set in alcoves separated by heavy carved screens and mirrors. The armchairs, upholstered in red figured frieze velvet, all swivel and are turned away from the tables to enable the passengers to sit down comfortably before rotating themselves to face their food. This kind of accommodation was one of the ultimate forms of the self-expression of a highly prosperous and confident age.

PLATE 68

The *Omrah* was a steel twin-screw steamship built at Glasgow in 1899 for the Orient Line service to Australia. She was of 8,000 tons and had accommodation for 350 people in the first and second classes and for 500 third class passengers. She was torpedoed in World War I.

The photograph shows the first class dining room, complete with organ, massive buffet and the long tables which persisted into the twentieth century. Again, the revolving chairs are marshalled to allow of easy use by people of both sexes in very formal dress – but they have become deformed, the backs shorter, the seats plumped-up, the arms ready to grab their occupants. It is interesting to compare this dining room with that in Plate 67. The opulence of the *Lucania*, built only six years earlier, has become grandiose vulgarity, the classical syntax is debased to mere jargon. The Ionic capitals look squashed while the columns themselves have a nasty texture – one suspects brown varnish – for two-thirds of their height. The upper storey is Town Hall Romanesque, the skylight above it assuming undue importance in the confidence that no heavy sea would ever reach the high midships structure where it stood. Only the lampshades have a natural gaiety – they would be collector's pieces now.

PLATE 69

The *Saxonia* was built in 1900 on the Clyde. Of 14,000 tons she was a steel twin-screw steamer and she spent twenty-five years on the North Atlantic route. On one of her earliest passages, the *Saxonia* crossed the Atlantic with 2,260 passengers – the largest number to have travelled from Britain to North America in one ship to that date. She had the reputation of being a remarkably steady vessel in a seaway.

This splendid photograph shows the vessel's first class smoking room. To enhance the illusion of being in an hotel on land the room has parquet flooring. Only the alleyway visible through the open door has any feeling of a ship about it. The decoration is markedly simpler than in the *Rome* twenty years before and the room looks comfortable and unpretentious. Oil lamps are still carried to back up the electric lighting in case of emergency.

PLATE 70

Compared with the accommodation offered in the first seventy years of the century, this second class cabin in the *Saxonia* represents luxury. It is considerably better than most first class accommodation a generation before and would not be out of place today. The washstands are developments of the mid-nineteenth century type already illustrated (Plate 61) and the handsome oil lamp backs up the electric light. The plaques on the guard rails bear the device of the Cunard Steamship Company Limited. The metal fittings are gleaming brass, which in the days before plastic lacquer had to be regularly cleaned and polished and this meant that labour was cheap. The bare metal deckhead and the berths one above the other left second class passengers in no doubt that they were at sea. First class passengers with their coffered ceilings could forget this if the motion of the vessel allowed.

PLATE 71

By way of further contrast with Plate 67, this photograph shows a third class smoking-room in the *Saxonia*. Even this austere compartment represents a considerable improvement on the emigrants' accommodation of forty years before, not the least of its benefits being the provision of a living space separate from the sleeping berths. It had the advantage that the simple fittings could be readily fumigated.

PLATE 72

This photograph taken on board the much larger *Aquitania*, built in 1914 on the Clyde, is included to give an impression of how the third class passengers in the *Saxonia* were accommodated. The dormitories of the sexes are segregated, the deckhand is high and the metal berths are permanent furniture. The trunking of the forced-draught ventilation system is visible and the metal side of the vessel is boarded off. The general arrangement, however, is still reminiscent of the accommodation shown in Plate 15 on board an emigrant ship of the 40s. But of course, for the passengers who slept here there were separate compartments to eat in, and for recreation, and a large covered deck area in which to stretch their legs. They also had washing and bathing places outside their accommodation and passably adequate water closets.

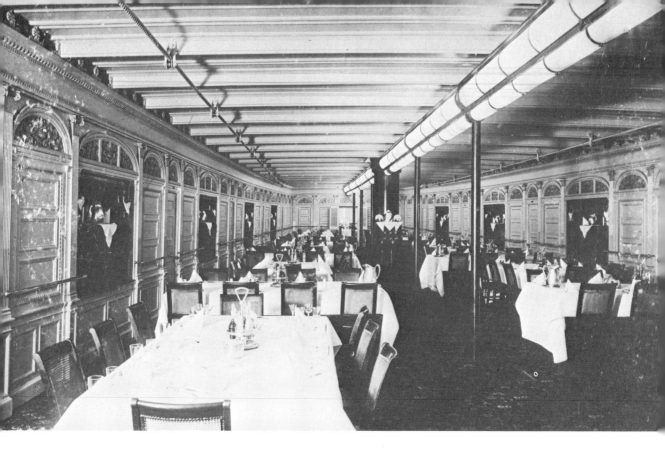

PLATE 73

The *Puritan* was a steel side-paddle steamer built in 1889, over one hundred feet long and at the time the largest vessel of its type ever built. She was launched for the famous Fall River Line and ran in Long Island Sound between New York City and Fall River, Massachusetts. She had the largest beam engine ever built and her 'walking beam' alone weighed 46 tons. Somewhat more simply fitted out in her accommodation than most of her predecessors, she was described as being decorated 'in the style of the Italian renaissance, the ornamentation being brought out by judicious gilding on an ivory-white ground'. While she was being built a contemporary writer recorded the view that she would be superb because 'the forests of both continents have been ransacked for choice wood for her interior'. A distinguished naval architect who specialised in side-wheeler design said that under way she was the most beautiful steamer of her day.

The photograph shows her main dining-room. True to North American river and short voyage steamer traditions it is a long open compartment not so very different from a big hotel dining-room ashore though more conservatively decorated than in many earlier steamers. The steering cables for the rudder can be seen slung from the deckhead on either side.

The *Puritan* was broken up in 1915.

PLATE 74

The *Priscilla*, another Fall River Line steamer, was built in 1894 and exceeded the *Puritan* in size. At the time she was built she was the largest side-wheel steamer in existence, more than 440 feet long and 93 feet wide. She carried 1,200 to 1,500 passengers. The photograph shows the main saloon looking aft from the stairway. A contemporary writer described it as like 'a concert hall in which there is ample room to seat 1,000 people'. It was 143 feet long and 30 feet wide. Thoroughly in the tradition of American steamers, it can be compared with the central saloon illustrated in Plate 46.

The *Priscilla* remained in service until the Fall River Line closed down in the 1930s.

PLATE 75

This photograph is of particular interest because although the vessel shown, the magnificent *Ticonderoga*, a Lake Champlain passenger steamer now preserved on dry land at the Shelburne Museum, Vermont, was built in 1906, the furniture is from earlier American steamers.

The photograph was taken in the *Ticonderoga's* stateroom hall, a covered deck surrounding the engine enclosure, which extends up through the vessel's three decks.

The fluted stanchions of cherry wood support the 'hurricane deck'. The settee is from the lake steamer *Vermont*, built in 1871, and the upholstery is the original upholstery of that date. The wood is walnut, hand-carved. Such chairs were designed to surround a mast, like those shown in the centre of the saloon of the *Priscilla* in the last plate. The single chair is from the steamer *Chateaugay*, built in 1898.

The *Ticonderoga*, which can be boarded by visitors to the Shelburne Museum, is the last survivor of the great era of the marine beam engine. She was built as a day steamer with only ten staterooms, but she could carry 1,200 people. She was 220 feet long – just half the size of the *Priscilla* – but even so she seems huge.

PLATE 76

The furniture in this cabin of the *Ticonderoga* is original, though the carpet is modern. The bed is of brass and the built-in washstand of cherry wood. The inevitable chamber pot is stowed in the right hand compartment of the cupboard. Notice the lifebelts slung above the bed head. The painting is of the *Jesse Hoyt*, built in 1862 at Keyport, New Jersey.

Paddle steamers working on the great rivers of East Pakistan offered first class passengers accommodation virtually indistinguishable from this as recently as the early 1960s.

PLATE 77

Photographs of the crew's accommodation in merchant steamships in the latter half of the
nineteenth century are even rarer than those taken in sailing vessels. The *Reliant* was built
on the Tyne in 1907 and is now preserved at the National Maritime Museum and is open to
visitors in the same way as the *Ticonderoga* at the Shelburne Museum. This photograph shows
her forecastle in which several men lived, though only for short periods in time. It compares
with similar accommodation in a small merchant steamship of the 1880s and 90s.

PLATE 78

The steamer *Marie Henriette* was built in Britain in 1893 for the Belgian government for a Dover–Ostend service. The standard of luxury for a short service passenger vessel is comparable to Queen Victoria's railway coach. This cabin, the King's Saloon, can indeed rarely, if ever, have been bettered for grandeur and comfort in the whole history of passenger accommodation at sea. Presumably the pedestal tables were bolted to the floor but the paraffin lamps must have been removed, unlit, to a place of safety in rough weather.

INDEX